SAILING PRIMER

SAILING PRIMER

by

W. D. PARK

*Director of Central Council
of Physical Recreation
Sailing Courses*

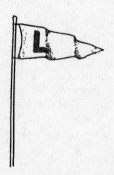

G. BELL & SONS, LTD
LONDON

A Bell Handbook

Printed in Great Britain by
The Camelot Press Ltd., London and Southampton

No ISBN

CONTENTS

Chapter 1

INTRODUCTORY

IT was in April that I bought my first sailing boat, a sloop named *Whimsy*—Bermudian rigged and clinker built at a cost of £120. This, be it noted, after due regard to the advice of old Captain Seaborne whose thirst at times seems quite insatiable, but is at least productive of sound advice. As he says, 'A boat be like a woman—'tis less expensive to keep a good un than a bad un—so choose right from the start and you'll have no regrets.'

Moreover, my bill of sale assures me that I own sixty-four sixty-fourths of *Whimsy* ('just in case she was previously owned by a syndicate and one part-owner be doing the selling unbeknown to t'others')—and further that she is free of all encumbrances. Who would have thought that the debts incurred in fitting out or repairing a boat can go with her to her new owner?

Much thinking, examining, knife probing and heart-burning, all thirst-making occupations, led to the choice of the craft. My first idea was to buy an old boat and 'do her up' myself during the winter. We looked at one such old boat most carefully. She was built over thirty years ago and as her owner said, 'They knew how to build boats in those days—and they used good seasoned timber not like these light cockle shells they sail to-day.'

She looked most pathetic and uncared for and I felt that I could have made much improvement to her with a bit of paint and varnish, but I realise the Captain was right, and he drank deeply in persuading me so. I now appreciate that wood $\frac{1}{2}$ inch thick alternately wet and dry and subject to the even quicker rotting action of fresh water in the bilges when the boat is laid up is bound to deteriorate in thirty years. Garboard strakes (the planks near the keel) had suffered most and are expensive to replace. The stem, the keel and the deadwoods were soft in places, the centre-board casing quite definitely leaked and a few timbers (ribs) were cracked *across* the grain, which is not at all good. The gaff-rigged mainsail is not as efficient as Bermudian, I'm told, and so though I could have bought her cheaply— say, for £40—I should have needed to spend perhaps another £20 on repairs, and even then would have been left with a boat comparatively inefficient by modern standards—and certainly difficult to sell again.

I next looked at a modern lightweight 14-footer beauti-fully built in waterproof plywood—with Bermudian rig— the whole boat only three years old and costing £130. Here is a type that could be towed by my little 8 h.p. car, and could be used on any inland waterway, as well as be taken on a tour of coastal resorts in the summer. The little craft weighs just over 2 cwt. and will ghost along in light airs, as well as being easily reefed in stronger winds. It's also a 'class' boat—one of hundreds all built to the same design and able to compete in races on equal terms.

Had there been only my wife and myself to consider— both of us keen and active—this would undoubtedly have been our boat now. I was sorely tempted, but reminded myself all the time that with the help only of my daughter aged twelve and the boy, Tony aged eleven, we might find launching a problem. Add to this the fact that my wife is rather more than timid where boats are concerned—and such light boats *do* capsize—that there would still be a road trailer to purchase (about £25) and a light launching trolly (about £8), and you will understand why I turned rather sadly from the boat; but I feel quite certain that in a few years' time when the boy and girl are in their middle teens this is the craft we will own, and they'll be able to race in regular competition and enjoy for life a sport second to none in exhilaration and hard competition—and how much better for them than a motor bike.

All things considered, I feel happy in my choice of *Whimsy*. She was built only six years ago and she'll comfortably take the four of us and leave us room to move about and picnic aboard when we reach the stage of estuary cruising. She is well equipped with good sails that should last two more seasons, an anchor and pair of paddles, and should we be caught out in a blow we have every reason for being confident that she'll get us safely back without falling to pieces.

With her full round bottom, she'll be very stable under sail as a family boat, and provided I remember to lift her centre-plate and rudder when I leave her on moorings, she'll sit upright on the mud if she dries out at low water—and float again just as happily on the flood tide. With her shallow draft she'll be able to negotiate quite shallow waters, giving us a chance to explore quiet creeks, without undue worries about a falling tide. When we run aground we can lift the plate a little and sail off again.

The Captain speaks learnedly about her Bermudian rig driving her close to windward on a beat, and no doubt I'll find out what he means as time goes on, but I like his quotation—probably a misquote: 'If you want a few hours of pleasure, get drunk—for a few days of happiness get married—but for a lifetime of pleasure, have a sailing boat.'

If costs and prices remain even moderately steady, then my boat can be expected to drop not more than £10 per year in value, and if I look after her really well she may even hold her value over two or three years. The Captain has worked out for me upkeep costs and it seems that these will average about 12s. per week for the year. The boat will spend her summer months on moorings to be hired from the local yard or the Harbour-master. The cost will be 3s. 6d. to 4s. per week from mid-April to mid-September, and will include the labour of keeping the boat pumped dry after heavy storms. Lifting the boat in and out will cost

£2 and winter storage ashore 2s. 6d. per week. I shall be quite prepared to do my own rubbing down, cleaning and painting and materials for this should cost me about £4. I am advised that a comprehensive Insurance policy will cost me £5 for the year, allowing six months in commission and six months laid up ashore.

A new set of sails in tough cotton would cost £25, but they can be expected to last for five years, and so I shall allow an average of £5 per year. The standing rigging in stainless steel should last for several years, but working on the principle that 'only the best is good enough' I shall replace all running rigging, halyards and sheets at least every other season, at an average cost per year of £3. I shall expect to need to replace occasionally a cleat, a bottle screw, a pulley block or a rudder pintle, and it is possible that the children may lose a rowlock or even a paddle. For these items I shall allow an average of £3 per year. My total annual expense therefore becomes about £30. The Captain assures me that if all the jobs were done for me in the yard, the bill would range from £50 to £75.

Of course, when I join the local Sailing Club I shall be able to lay her up ashore on the Club premises at a cheaper rate, enjoy the free use of the Club derrick for lifting the boat in and out each season and eventually when the children graduate to a class racer like the Hornet or '505' they'll have the use of the Club ramp and dinghy park.

But we're still in the present. To-morrow we go aboard the good ship—and have our first sailing lesson.

I'm secretly glad to think of the built-in buoyancy tanks fitted discreetly under the thwarts so that if we *should* capsize the boat will remain afloat though waterlogged, providing us with a little island of safety until the Captain can get us out of trouble.

Chapter 2

FIRST SAILING SESSION

I AM already a day late with my log, but last night we were all so tired we could do little more than talk ecstatically about the virtues of *Whimsy*, compare the blisters on our hands, and wonder how we got so many bruises, before going wearily to bed.

We went aboard in the early morning. The Captain was waiting for us by a little pulling dinghy on the slip-way and while rowing across gave us the most serious warnings about our behaviour aboard. It seems that a boat has the heart of a most sensitive lady, and must be treated with respect. No word of criticism concerning her appearance or her sailing ability must be uttered while enjoying her hospitality. No slighting reference may be made to the shortsightedness of her designer or the hamfisted faults of her builder. Under harsh criticism she'll sulk, and in the words of the Captain, 'If you call her an old sea-cow she'll undoubtedly behave like one.'

Praise, compliments and encouragement are called for aboard, and criticism of a constructive kind should take the form of 'We'll give you a much nicer coat of varnish than this for next season' or 'You shall have a really superior quality paint when you're fitted out again'.

Firmness and hard driving will certainly be called for on occasion, but preferably when boat and crew are well known to one another. (Something of the ignorance or impatience or dissatisfaction of Helmsman and crew is often reflected, I think, in the way they sail.)

Arriving aboard, we bade *Whimsy* 'Good morning', made

fast our rowing-boat painter to her mooring rope, put her mooring buoy aboard the rowing boat, and proceeded with our starting drill. It already seems quite simple. First we lowered the centre-plate, and as it is operated by block and tackle even Tony was able to raise and lower it for practice several times, though the iron plate must weigh nearly 1 cwt. We each repeated the operation to make sure

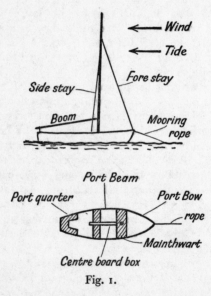

Fig. 1.

of it. Next, the rudder-plate was lowered down to its working position. This was quite easily arranged with a piece of stout cord that fitted on a cleat. The tiller was put into the head of the rudder and that unit became ready for action. We examined the anchor rope, made sure that it was tied securely to the ring bolt in the bows, coiled it down carefully right-handed (clockwise) and laid the anchor on top of it all ready for use at a moment's notice.

We then observed the direction of wind and tide and noted that they were in the easiest position for us—both moving in the same direction, so that the bows of the boat headed into wind and tide together (*Fig. 1*).

Now from the bag we had carried aboard we drew out the mainsail and the smaller triangular jib. The foot of the mainsail was fitted with slides that travelled along a track on the boom. We fixed it tightly at each end according

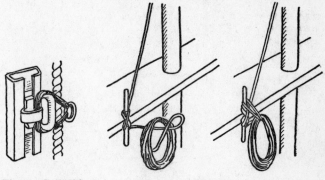

Fig. 2*a*. Sail slide
   seized to luff.

Fig. 2*b*.

to instructions. The leading edge of the mainsail—the tall vertical side of it—the luff—was also fitted with brass slides which slid into a track (*Fig. 2a*) running almost for the full height of the mast on the aft side (facing the stern). The main halyard ran from a belaying pin near the foot of the mast over a pulley block at the mast-head, and down again to working level where the end was fixed to a shackle in the head of the sail. By hauling on the loose end, or the 'fall', of this halyard, we hoisted the mainsail, taking care to lift the boom as we did so. We now seemed to have yards and yards of spare main halyard about our feet and this was coiled neatly and hung on its correct belaying pin (*Fig. 2b*).

The sail flapped vigorously and the boom swung to and fro in a most menacing fashion, but following the Captain's example we remained outwardly calm and ignored it. Then in turn the three of us, Tony, Ann, and myself practised hoisting the sail, coiling the halyard and hanging it

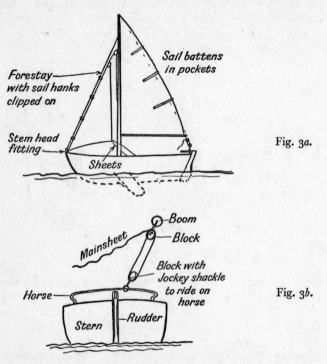

Sail battens
in pockets

Forestay
with sail hanks
clipped on

Stem head
fitting

Sheets

Fig. 3a.

Boom

Block

Mainsheet

Block with
Jockey shackle
to ride on
horse

Horse

Fig. 3b.

Stern   Rudder

neatly on a pin, until each one of us knew just how to carry out this job. In a similar fashion we hoisted the small triangular jib or foresail. Along its leading edge were stitched small pistol-grip fittings that clipped over the wire forestay. The bottom of the sail was shackled to the stem-head in the bows, while the peak was hauled up, not quite to the mast head, by a jib halyard. The fall was coiled and hung on a cleat side by side with the main halyard.

Again we practised in turn until each one of us was able to carry out the correct sail hoisting procedure. Now the jib sheets (the ropes which control its movement on either side of the boat), were threaded through the appropriate fairleads and led to positions at each side of the boat just behind, sorry, *aft* of the mast (*Fig. 3a*). At this stage the jib was flapping so vigorously that it was taken down while we continued our exploration of the boat. The mainsheet, a very long rope to control the boom—and so to control the mainsail—passed through pulley blocks on the horse and on the boom in order to give sufficient mechanical advantage to allow the helmsman to hold it against the pull of the wind (*Fig. 3b*). Finally, we tied to each side-stay, at a point as high as we could reach, a piece of coloured wool that immediately blew out on the wind and was to act as our 'tell-tale' to give us a rough idea of wind direction at all times.

Later we will have our own burgee hoisted to the mast-head and this will give us an even better indication, but I gather that the Captain is very fond of those bits of wool which can be seen at a glance without taking your eyes far away from the direction in which you may be travelling at any time.

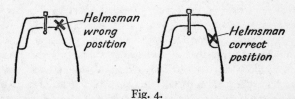

Fig. 4.

Now we took up our sailing positions and I was appointed helmsman. I immediately sat proudly and very self-consciously right back in the stern corner of the boat with my arm resting along the tiller-stick—the position I have seen so frequently in pictures. The Captain growled

B

something about 'that position being reserved for film-stars and quite unsuited for a helmsman'—and made me move forward to one side of the boat so that I was in a position to move the tiller completely in either direction without having myself in the way of it (*Fig. 4*).

The main mooring rope was untied except for one turn through the eye-bolt in the bows, and young Tony went forward to hold this until he was instructed to cast off. The Captain pointed out that we could sail roughly at 45° to either side of our present position lying head to wind and tide. If we were to sail to starboard—the right side looking from my position at the tiller—then we would sail into the shore and so obviously we must decide to turn the boat's bow to the left (port) and sail away in that direction. I could see that once we had turned into this sailing position, then the wind would be coming over the starboard side of the boat and I was instructed to sit to windward of my tiller—on the starboard side.

Young Ann now took charge of both jib sheets and by pulling hard on the starboard sheet hauled the foot of the jib across in that direction; it caught the wind and we could see that it tended to turn our bows to port. She immediately let go and the boat came back to position head to wind. The Captain sat just in front of me, gave the word to young Tony to let go the mooring rope, while Ann at the same time backed the jib to starboard as before to turn the boat's head to port. Quite gently we were away. Ann was told to let go the starboard sheet and pull tightly on the port sheet of the jib. We immediately began to sail much more briskly in the direction we had planned and with a word or two from the Captain about pulling the tiller towards me or pushing it away from me, we slipped easily past neighbouring moored boats and came to a wide stretch of open water. Here our real training began (*Fig. 5*).

Ann continued to look after both jib sheets. Tony came aft to sit near me, and he took charge of the mainsheet, while I, for the first time in my life, steered my own boat on a given course. The hulk of an old boat lying ashore at the far side of the estuary became my leading mark and I juggled with the tiller in order to keep the bows of the boat pointing all the time at my mark. Occasionally when the wind blew more strongly the bows of the boat would swing away from the mark up into the wind, and only gradually did I learn to correct this smoothly on the tiller instead of with sudden jerky movements, each leading to

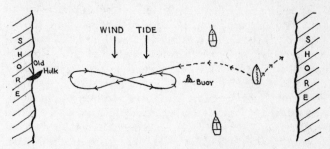

Fig. 5. Sailing a broad reach.

(This and similar diagrams in the book are not drawn to scale.)

another one in the opposite direction. I gradually learnt to avoid gripping the tiller as though I were about to use it as a weapon and instead merely to press with my fingers against the normal pull of the rudder. As we approached our mark we were given instructions for turning round to come back on a course that would be practically re-tracing our steps. Instructions were repeated and when eventually the Captain said, 'Ready to go about'—pause—'The helm's a-lee', I pushed the tiller down wind (away from me) and remained seated while I watched the bows of the boat turn up towards the wind, and continue to swing in the same arc until the boom was fore and aft and just starting to swing towards me; then I ducked underneath, took up my new position directly opposite on the port side and played with the tiller to bring the boat's head on to our new leading mark, a small black and white buoy quite close to our original mooring.

Meanwhile Ann had been carrying out an apparently complicated manœuvre with the jib that I came to understand only later. We were interested in the origins of our commands for going about and could well appreciate that after the first warning—'Ready to go about', there must be a pause while sheets on a big windjammer are freed from their cleats, then when the helmsman gives his action signal 'The helm's a-lee' everybody knows the ship is going to turn into the wind and swing round to her new course. Later when the Captain rather sadly said we could abbreviate our command to 'Ready about—Lee Ho' I was a little disappointed and determined to keep to the rolling cadence of the older expression. Approaching the black and white buoy I repeated this over and over in my mind, and called out the first words, 'Ready to go about'. When we were fairly near to the buoy, all took action on the final words 'The helm's a-lee'. I ducked under the boom, changing sides with it, and took up my original position on the starboard side, and we were 'about', sailing on our first course again, heading for the old hulk. In fact we spent the whole morning sailing on this figure of eight course, always with the wind a-beam—'sailing on a broad reach' it's called. In turn we had charge of the tiller, the jib and the mainsheet. Soon I had an opportunity of learning the technique of going about on the jib and we all learnt to do this the hard way, ready for any emergency. When with the jib hauled to starboard I heard the command 'The helm's a-lee', I let the sheet go free until the bows of the boat were pointing into the wind and the jib itself was fluttering in a direct line to the mast. At that stage I gave another firm tug on the same sheet to back the jib and force round the bows of the boat in the same way we had used for leaving our moorings—but this only momentarily until I heard the boom swing to its new position. Then I let go completely on the starboard sheet and hauled firmly on the port sheet. The Captain assured us that this manœuvre will not normally be necessary, but in light airs or in a choppy sea we may save getting 'in stays' if we use our technique of backing the jib; it is something worth knowing thoroughly in order to be ready for the type of emergency that may arise.

Ann proved a most efficient helmsman and I was filled with admiration. When Tony's turn came he was even better and we could see how the constant repetition of instruction was having an effect on all of us.

I enjoyed my turns as mainsheet hand, and could feel how I helped to drive the boat up into the wind by hauling on the mainsheet when going about.

After an hour we had each enjoyed twenty minutes at every job, and had almost ploughed our private shipping lane between the old hulk and the black and white buoy; we could all sail that course efficiently, could hold the tiller gently but steadily and only on one occasion did the Captain look back at a zigzag wake and remark that if a big sea serpent was following us now, he'd break his blooming back!

It seemed an easy progressive step to take when the Captain decreed that the helmsman should hold the main-sheet as well as the tiller, and so our duties were quietly altered. The helmsman took mainsheet and tiller, one hand looked after the jib completely, and the third hand merely concentrated on moving across the boat so as always to sit 'to weather' (on the windward side) and help to balance her against the thrust of the wind; whoever had this job acted as moving ballast in fact and needed to be remarkably agile in ducking under the boom and stepping over the centre-plate box while the boat was 'going about'.

As helmsman my attention was fully occupied in con-trolling the tiller to hold our course as already practised and in grasping the mainsheet firmly to keep the sail well filled without any trace of flapping in the luff; yet at the same time I had to be prepared to 'ease' the mainsheet—to spill some wind—when a sudden gust struck us, causing the boat to heel in rather an alarming fashion until I mastered this dual technique. Alarming did I say?—the children loved it, and so did I after a while.

And now also the jibsheet hand—foredeck hand—was allowed to 'make fast' the jib sheet on its special cleat and our blisters did not really mature as they might have done.

It was most interesting when going about near the black and white buoy to note the effect of the tide and I felt glad to be learning on a tidal estuary, yet this tide effect is somewhat disconcerting and I shall be glad to know more about it. But, as the Captain said, 'It's good to play with one piece of the jig-saw puzzle at a time.' When we know *all* the pieces, we'll have a full picture and we'll then be sailors.

Before finishing our first session we all knew the meaning of such comments as 'Keep her steady as she goes'. This involved gentle movements on the tiller to keep the boat's *bows* steady on course. When given such a command we were at first inclined merely to hold the tiller steady—and the bows quickly veered off course.

'Luff up' or 'Come closer' meant bringing the bows

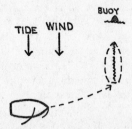

Fig. 6. Fore reaching to a buoy.

closer to the wind direction by pushing the tiller 'down wind', while 'bearing away' meant directing the bows still farther away from the wind by pulling the tiller 'up wind'.

Before returning to our moorings we put in several

practice runs as though we were about to pick up the black and white buoy. While steering a course that would carry us a good boat's length to the leeward side of the buoy (down wind, 'to loo'ward' of the buoy) with the wind over the port beam, we would turn firmly up into the wind and allow the momentum of the boat—the 'way' of the boat—to carry us up to the buoy with the boat's head pointing directly into the wind and all sails fluttering (*Fig. 6*). Gradually we learnt to gauge this manœuvre so that we could nudge gently with our bows against the mooring buoy. In exactly this way did we return and pick up our own moorings and make fast. We left all sails aboard ready for our afternoon session, and went religiously through our drill.

1. Mooring really made fast (two half hitches) and mooring buoy aboard.
2. Mooring rope in the fairlead in the bows.
3. Centre-plate up.
4. Rudder-plate up.
5. Boom lashed.
6. Sails lashed.
7. Boat pumped dry.

Then thanking *Whimsy* for a most happy morning we were rowed ashore by Ann and Tony, taking rather a long time over it, but arriving eventually. And what an amazing number of things we had learned in less than three hours. Even a point concerning buoys may well be useful some day. The deep-water channel in an estuary is indicated to the helmsman by buoys. Coming from *seaward* he must leave red, flat-topped, can-shaped buoys to port and black conical buoys to starboard.

Chapter 3

SECOND SAILING SESSION

By afternoon the tide had turned, but the wind remained steady, and *Whimsy* was lying broadside, affected equally by the wind to starboard, and tide to port. Tony and Ann rowed us aboard and we made our rowing boat fast to the mooring as before.

Starting drill was quickly repeated: centre-plate, rudder-plate, tiller, but after unlashing sails we paused for a moment to consider the directions of wind and tide as they would affect us in sailing away from the moorings. If we hoisted the mainsail it would billow out over our port beam and the boom, of necessity, would also have to swing wide to port (*Fig. 7*). It would be awkward to hold up the boom

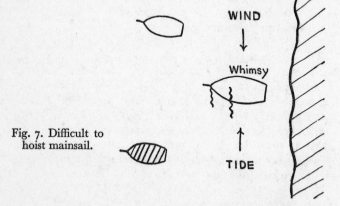

Fig. 7. Difficult to hoist mainsail.

while the sail was hoisted, to take the initial weight of the sail, and further, the slides in the sail would be liable to

jam in the track on the mast. We felt that hoisting the
mainsail under such conditions would be extremely difficult, and decided to sail away on the jib only. Tony
hoisted it, but for this session the Captain wanted the luff
of the jib to be as taut as possible, and introduced us to the
technique of 'swigging' on a rope.

With the sail hauled up and the halyard turned only once
round the belaying pin, we pulled aft on the standing part
of the rope, gaining more purchase than if we merely
pulled downwards on the halyard, and then snatched an
extra couple of inches round the pin as we let go on the
standing part (*Fig. 8*).

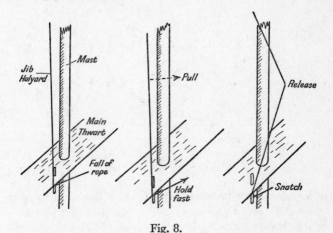

Fig. 8.

This, repeated, gave us a very tight halyard and consequently a very firm luff to the jib. Then the halyard was
made fast, figure-of-eight fashion, with the fall coiled and
hung from the pin.

I took my place at the tiller. Ann went forward to cast
off the mooring rope, and Tony prepared to control the
jib sheets, though as yet they were both flapping wildly.
When Ann cast off, I pulled the tiller up wind, Tony

hauled on the port jib sheet just sufficiently to keep the sail well filled and the bows swung to port, until we were running quietly and very slowly over the tide with a well-filled jib just taking us along (*Fig. 9*). As we made our way

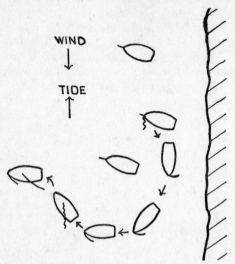

Fig. 9. Leaving under jib.

to a point where we could turn up into the wind in open water Ann prepared for a rapid hoisting of the mainsail. When she was quite ready and I could look round and find no obstructions to sea room, I pushed the tiller hard away from me and we rounded up almost head into the wind, for the few seconds that Ann needed to hoist the mainsail in the normal way.   Her swigging on the rope was not very efficient but with the help from Tony she managed quite well and soon we were sailing on a broad reach and aiming for the old hulk.

Now we tried a series of experiments concerned with the angle at which the wind flowed over the sails on different

points of sailing (*Fig. 10*).   With both sails just filled without trembling at the luff, Tony's jib sheet made fast, and

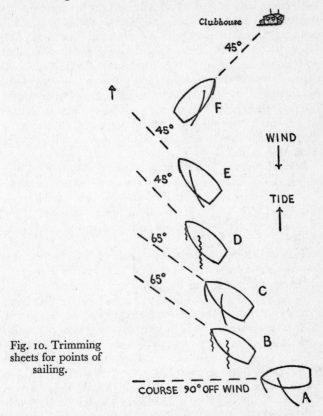

Fig. 10. Trimming
sheets for points of
sailing.

my mainsheet held quite steady, *Whimsy* at 'A' sailed briskly
on a broad reach—course 90°.   Then I pushed the tiller
gently away from me and very gradually came closer to the
wind till we were at 'B', pointing on course 65° with the
wind directly in line with our sails—now flapping uselessly.
The boat had ceased to drive forward at all.   We continued

to point on course 65° but the sails merely fluttered and we drifted on the tide. Now we hauled in the sheets until again both sails were well filled without any trace of flapping in the luff and found that we were driving strongly forward, position 'C' on course 65°. We repeated this manœuvre. I pushed down the tiller gently until I had *Whimsy* at 'D', pointing on course 45°. Again we noted that the wind was simply blowing *along* our sails and we were no longer driving forward. We hauled in both jib and mainsheet to the utmost this time (Position 'E'). *Whimsy* heeled sharply and seemed positively to rush forward on course 45°— sheets close hauled—and the boat sailing as close to the wind as possible.

I found that my 'mark' was a distant post with a triangle on top of it. In a moment we went about as we had practised so often before, but this time without backing the jib ('F'). Our new course was again at an angle of 45° to the wind and my new mark was the distant Club House.

This zigzag progress against the wind is called tacking. We continued our experiments and found that if I went still closer to the wind, the leading edge of the sail flapped vigorously, and we ceased to drive forward. With some practice and careful observation of the position of our 'telltale' wind indicator, which was blowing almost parallel with the sail or only slightly towards it, we gradually learned to sail in this close hauled position. We were travelling against the wind (i.e. beating to windward) close hauled on a port tack (i.e. with the wind over the port bow) with jib sheet and mainsheet hauled in as tightly as they would come. Our speed seemed greater than anything before, the boat heeled and felt alive, and as we butted into the wavelets built up by wind against tide, they broke in cascades of flying spray over our weather bows. The sun scattered diamonds on the broken water, the wind was fresh on my face and I found a new exhilaration.

We tacked to a point from where we could see ahead of

us the red and white Fairway buoy (*Fig. 11*). I left this about two boat lengths away on my starboard beam while beating on a port tack, when the Captain ordered me to 'Bear away'. I pulled the tiller towards me and at the

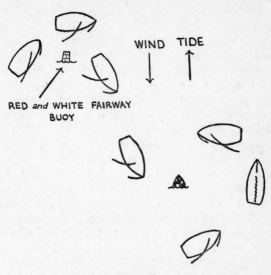

Fig. 11.

same time was ordered to ease the mainsheet while Tony eased the jib. We turned through a broad reach and continued turning to a course where the wind was over our port quarter, not dead astern, but slightly to port of that direction. The jib and mainsail were well out over the starboard beam, and we were running back to our first sailing area. The Captain instructed me to leave the black and white buoy on my port side. This I did, allowing a boat's length between *Whimsy* and the buoy. Then, still acting on instructions, I held course for two boat lengths beyond the buoy before rapidly hauling in the mainsheet while Tony hauled in his jib sheet, to sail close hauled on a port tack with the wind coming over the port bow—again beating to windward.

In actual fact we were almost back where we started, and I proceeded to go over the same course again beating to windward—tacking on a zigzag course that took me round the red and white buoy, then bearing away and running back with the wind over the port quarter. Again I rounded the black and white buoy, leaving it to port, not going so far beyond it this time yet allowing a boat length to provide for the drift of the tide before I rounded up into the wind again. Tony and Ann each took their turn and we all came to understand the various points of sailing we had covered. Finally, we went over the various sailing points and terms in general use.

At point A, beating to windward, close hauled on a starboard tack—wind over the starboard bow, I was called upon to bear away (*Fig. 12*). I pulled the tiller slightly towards me, eased out a little mainsheet, and we reached position B. On this course we were sailing free—that is free and able if necessary to sail closer to the wind in a close hauled position or free also to bear away still more. In fact, we were sailing 'full and bye.' Next, I was told to bear away even more until I was on a broad reach, position C. Here was a familiar point of sailing, the wind over the beam, the boom eased out until the sail was filled but not trembling. Then came the word to bear away yet again to position D, where we were running with the wind over the quarter—probably our fastest point of sailing though it didn't feel like it. At this stage, we tried going about without using the tiller at all—simply hauling in the mainsheet steadily and firmly to drive our boat up into the wind through the normal arc and on to a new course. This seemed rather good planning to me because when you're hauling in the mainsheet with both hands, it's difficult to hold the tiller as well.

Ann and Tony each insisted on making sure of these points individually and then we considered how best to

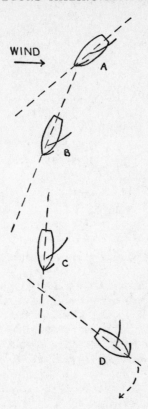

WIND

Fig. 12. Points of sailing.

return and pick up our mooring (*Fig. 13*). If we luffed up into the wind as we had done this morning, then we would still have the tide under us to surge us forward at two or three knots and might find it difficult to hold on to our mooring buoy. We might even bump rather violently into our little rowing boat waiting for us on the mooring. We agreed that it would be better to sail to the windward side of our moored rowing boat, luff up into the

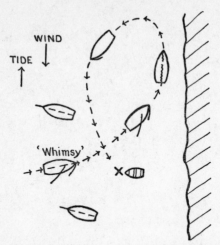

Fig. 13. Picking up mooring under jib only.

wind, drop the mainsail while the boom was still fore and aft in the boat then swing round to port and return to our mooring under jib only, knowing that this would hold enough wind to carry us slowly over the tide, in the same way as we had left moorings a couple of hours earlier. This manœuvre worked very easily and soon we were ashore and glancing back to catch a last glimpse of *Whimsy* riding contentedly on her moorings after a day that every one of us had thoroughly enjoyed.

Tony looked every inch a tough sailor as he strode along with the sail bag over his shoulder, his hair and clothes wet with spray and an expression of rapt satisfaction on his face.

If only I could have had this training at his age.   As it is I'll want to play truant from work whenever the sun shines and the gulls have enough wind for soaring.

Chapter 4

THIRD SAILING SESSION

GALES and rain yesterday kept us ashore for the day, and I was glad of a chance to write up my notes. The youngsters were absorbed in making a model of *Whimsy* and manœuvring her through every possible gyration, while the Captain assured me he would be happily and completely occupied ensuring that we had an empty bottle to carry aboard for our next session afloat. It turned out to be an essential part of our equipment.

When we started again to-day we were blessed with sunshine and a steady breeze that had veered to a different quarter. As we walked along the quayside, we sighted *Whimsy* from some little distance away, bobbing at her mooring with every sign of impatience as she waited for us. There were literally dozens of other craft in the anchorage, but we had eyes for none of them: they merely provided a setting for our own gem. Our pace quickened as we discussed her virtues until on reaching the slipway Tony was almost trotting under his sailbag, Ann already fastening her lifejacket and the Captain well in the lead, the smell of his tobacco not too unpleasant on the morning air.

In spite of our haste to be aboard, we allowed Ann to row us across to the mooring and Tony in his impatience knelt in front of her with a hand on each paddle to lend some extra power to her pulling. Aboard, everything was wet and we spent a few minutes wiping down, laughing at the same time as we remembered that a soaking with seaspray hadn't worried us in the slightest, but we were loath to sit on rain-wet seats. We were glad to have dry sails, and resolved that always, no matter how tired we might be at the end of a day's sailing, we would still take the trouble to unbend sails and carry them away with us. There was much water in the bilges, and after we had pumped dry we all moved aft, lifted the floor-board in the stern and baled out the final bucketful. Sailing drill went ahead rapidly then and we were soon ready for hoisting sails. At this stage, as had now become our habit, we looked round carefully and considered how to leave the mooring (*Fig. 14a*).

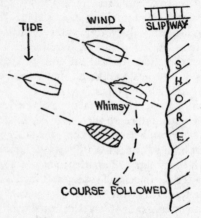

Fig. 14a. Leaving moorings.

The tide was low, leaving *Whimsy* very close to the shore, and to make it even more difficult the wind was blowing across the tide directly towards our side of the estuary, giving us a lee shore just a few yards away, while a strange boat was riding at anchor to windward of us. If we drifted ashore we would have to lift the centre-plate and then the rudder-plate, and might be driven firmly aground to be faced with a really difficult job in getting away again. Our great concern was to ensure that when starting to sail we must keep going, and in the right direction.

We knew we could sail at an angle of 45° to the wind and in considering this we were loath to leave on a port tack because of a cement barge aground at the nearby slipway which blocked the narrow channel there.   On a starboard tack we wondered if we might clear the bows of the black dinghy moored fairly near us, but allowing for the tide carrying us in her direction, we realised we must go under her stern rather than risk being so close to her bows that our centre-plate could catch on her submerged mooring rope.   It was fairly easy to set all sail while on the mooring

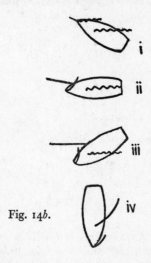

Fig. 14*b*.

and we made sure that luffs were really tight by swigging on both the halyards before making fast.   We knew now to leave sheets quite free while we were still on the mooring, and although there was a terrific pandemonium of flapping canvas, this didn't last for long.   We took up our positions with Tony at the tiller, as he had never taken us from moorings before, Ann at the jib and I ready to cast off our mooring (*Fig. 14b(i)*).   When the helmsman gave us the word Ann

backed the jib to starboard to turn our bows to port (*ii*).
I pulled hand over hand on the mooring rope and carried
it aft to the side stays, where for a moment before I let go it
seemed that we were held almost broadside to the wind (*iii*);
then Ann had the jib drawing to port, Tony kept the main
well filled, and we were suddenly driving strongly with the
tide (*iv*), to pass close under the stern of the black dinghy
well clear of that lee shore. And so we sailed away without
mishap, leaving the black boat comfortably to starboard.
We tacked across to our sailing area beyond the black and
white buoy and were ready for further instruction.

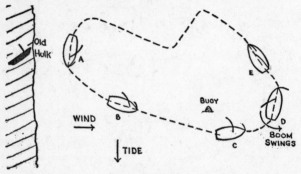

Fig. 15. Gybing.

I took the helm, gave the word to 'bear away' (*Fig. 15, A*)
near the old hulk and with the wind over the starboard
quarter (*B*) ran towards the black and white buoy. On the
way we all listened carefully to instructions for 'gybing'.
I left the buoy a boat length to port and ran beyond it for
two more lengths (*C*). Then on the command 'Ready to
gybe', Ann released the jib sheet. On 'Gybe-O' she let
go the sheet, while I pulled up the tiller hard towards me
(*D*), held it in that position with my hip, and hauled in the
mainsheet hand over hand, being careful to leave it all in a
heap just in front of me. I watched the boom carefully,

and as it suddenly lifted slightly and swung hard over my head across the boat, I let all the mainsheet run out quite freely to swish through the blocks as the boom rushed out over the starboard beam, when I moved quickly across to the port side, so releasing my tiller. Without worrying at all about the tiller, I picked up my mainsheet, hauled it in rapidly hand over hand, and grabbed the tiller again only as we came into a close hauled position (*E*) beating to windward on a port tack with jib and main close hauled. Here was a new way of turning the boat round, vastly different from going about head into the wind—apparently very much quicker—and certainly more exciting with so much vigorous action and so many things to think about.

I tacked across towards the old hulk again until I could conveniently bear away and start a second run to gybe round the buoy. This time I remembered to watch the boom and also to spare glances at the wind 'tell-tale' and ahead over the bows to pick up my new course more precisely.

We all practised gybing until we could turn *Whimsy* almost in her own length, to the music of the swish of sheet racing through blocks, with scarcely a jolt to the boat as she swung round before heeling steadily on her new course.

After a while we were able to make really tight gybing turns, fairly close to the buoy on the approach and a little farther away to allow for the tide when we rounded up into our beat.

We had our mishaps, of course, and realised that if the mainsheet should jam in a strong wind, become tangled round the helmsman's feet, or snarled up on any obstruction, then we should be broadside to the wind, and having little forward momentum at the time might suffer capsizing.

And so invariably our crew practised moving rapidly across under the boom to balance the boat, even before the helmsman did so.

It seems clear now that if we put up the tiller to gybe round from a run while the boom is wide over the beam, and

if we don't haul in the mainsheet, then we reach a position
where the wind will sweep the mainsail with increasing
speed across the boat and to the opposite side, carrying
everything before it—and possibly break our sidestays
supporting the mast. By hauling in the mainsheet quickly
to control the boom, then releasing the mainsheet and allowing it to rush through the blocks as the boom swings in a
controlled fashion across the boat, we reduce the danger of
this manœuvre to negligible proportions. I understand
from the Captain that our technique is the most effective
for our particular craft with a fairly long boom at the foot
of the sail, and depends to a great extent on our having a
mainsheet that runs easily through the blocks. On any
other boat we sail we may have to learn this manœuvre
afresh. On light racing dinghies the boom will be held
down by a kicking strap. The boom will be very short in
relation to the height of the sail, the mainsheet will probably
run less easily through very light blocks, and the general
technique will be slightly different. We won't need to
haul in quite so vigorously in order to ease out smoothly,
while the time factor in racing will lead us to take more risk
during this manœuvre and rely on helmsman and crew
moving quickly to windward, to balance the boat when the
boom swings. All this just to remind me of future possibili-
ties, but the crew of *Whimsy* must know the technique she
prefers, and we'll adhere to this while we sail her, though, of
course, we shall experiment at a later date.

When next it was my trick at the helm we practised a drill
for picking up a man overboard (*Fig. 16*). During a run
with the wind on the starboard quarter, the Captain dropped
the bottle over the side, called out 'Man overboard', and
directed Tony to watch the bottle carefully throughout all
subsequent manœuvres. I gybed round to a close hauled
course, went about for a little way, then luffed up with the
bottle under my port bow, the tide drifting me to it for Tony
to pick up. If he had not constantly kept an eye on it and
indicated where it floated I should certainly have lost all

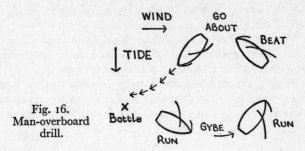

Fig. 16.
Man-overboard
drill.

sense of direction during this manœuvre. For the next half-hour we picked up the bottle a dozen times and on each occasion the helmsman was timed. According to our speed in gybing round, coming on to the wind and luffing up to rescue the man overboard, we found that such an unfortunate could be in the water for 25 seconds—or very much longer.

We next timed our man overboard drill using different tactics (*Fig. 17*). Again on a run, we heard the call 'Man

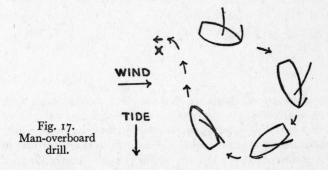

Fig. 17.
Man-overboard
drill.

overboard' but this time we rounded up into the wind by hauling in our sheets, to a course beating close hauled to windward, then went about on a new tack and so came to the bottle. We found that this method generally took slightly longer, but could be more certain, and would be safer than gybing in rough weather.

We spent some time gybing round from a broad reach and even from a close hauled position but after our previous experience these operations seemed quite easy.

Finally we made several dummy runs on the black and white buoy in preparation for picking up our mooring with wind blowing across the tide. We found the best method

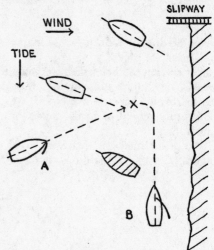

Fig. 18.
Picking up moorings.
A, jib only.
B, mainsail only.

was to approach under full sail on a broad reach with the wind over the port beam, on a course that would take us nearly two full boat lengths to loo'ard of the buoy, rounding up into the wind to forereach or carry our way to a position where the buoy would be just under our port bow. The tide did the rest for us and carried us gently on to the buoy.

This was most effective, but as we made for our own mooring where our rowing boat was made fast, we realised there wasn't room to carry out such a manœuvre. We had a

clear run for an approach under jib only (*Fig. 18, A*), but
as we already knew this method, we tried the slightly more
difficult one under mainsail only (*B*).   On a broad reach
against the tide, we eased the mainsheet gradually to spill wind
and control speed, until we luffed up very gently alongside
the rowing boat—'without crushing an egg'.   As we rowed
ashore, the Captain assured us we had practised almost
every manœuvre and point of sailing that mattered at this
stage and were now ready to 'go foreign', or at least sail
round a triangular course, in the afternoon.

Chapter 5

FOURTH SAILING SESSION

WHEN next we rowed out to our mooring in the afternoon to prepare *Whimsy* for sailing, we found that the tide had turned, and as we looked round to sum up the situation, it seemed that we had two alternatives for getting under way (*Fig. 19a*). Our position was affected by both wind and tide—we were partly 'wind-rode' and partly 'tide-rode'. The wind was fine over our starboard bow and it seemed

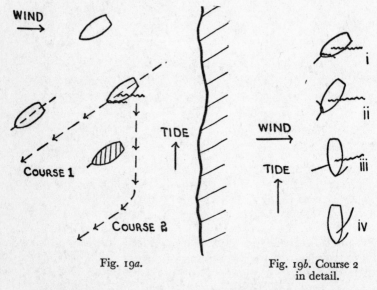

Fig. 19a.

Fig. 19b. Course 2 in detail.

that by hardening our sheets we could fairly easily sail clear of the anchorage on Course 1, perhaps putting in a short tack on the way. Ever anxious to try the more difficult things while we had the Captain with us, we chose the alternative, Course 2, and it was Ann's turn on the tiller. She left the mainsheet free while Tony backed the jib to starboard for a moment to turn our bows to port (*b, ii*), and at the same time I hauled our mooring rope towards the starboard side-stay—almost amidships—to turn *Whimsy* broadside to the wind without allowing her to drift at all towards the lee shore (*iii*). Tony quickly let the jib draw to port, Ann hauled in the mainsheet to keep the sail just comfortably filled and we were away (*iv*), reaching against the tide with the wind over our starboard beam to a point where we could clear the black boat and beat across to the windward or weather side of the estuary. Here we went through the points of sailing with the wind direction any-where from abeam to astern, i.e. aft of the beam—or abaft the beam.

Quite near the weather bank we turned into a broad reach with the wind over the port beam (*Fig. 20, A*). Then we were given the word to bear away until we were running with the wind over the port quarter (*B*). By bearing away still more we ran with the wind directly over our stern, but now the jib was completely blanketed by the mainsail and so we set it out on the opposite side of the boat and sailed along with a 'goosewing' effect: jib out to port and mainsail wide to starboard (*C*). We noticed a certain amount of rolling and understood that a 'rhythmic roll' is quite usual when running with the wind dead aft. We continued to turn even more until the wind was slightly starboard of our stern (*D*). Both sails remained well filled, as before, but the tiller lost some of its feeling of firm-ness and needed such light movements that it conveyed a feeling of insecurity. In this position we were sailing 'by the lee' where a sudden wind shift could sweep our boom across the boat to cause an involuntary gybe: a gybe 'all-standing'. While I appreciate that the position may be taken as a calculated risk in the heat of racing, even to the

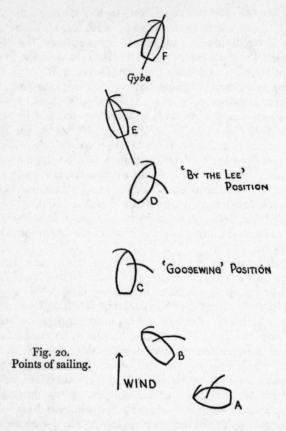

Gybe

'By the Lee'
Position

'Goosewing' Position

Fig. 20.
Points of sailing.

WIND

extent of having the crew lean on the boom to hold it down
and enable the skipper to avoid a change of course before
rounding a mark, I still feel that such efforts will be no concern of mine for some time.   I was glad when we luffed a
little to run with the wind over the quarter (*E*) in a normal
way, and we all agreed that on a long run with the wind
astern it would be safer to choose a slightly zigzag course
putting in an occasional voluntary gybe (*F*) to make sure

that the wind was always over the quarter. Certainly in a strong wind there would be considerable risk attached to gybing all-standing without being prepared.

We took turns at the helm to try these various points of running before the wind, and during each return to the weather side of the estuary practised man overboard drill while beating to windward.

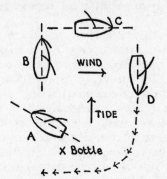

Fig. 21.
'Wearing' ship.

With *Whimsy* on a port tack (*Fig. 21, A*), the bottle was dropped overboard. The helmsman immediately called to the free member of the crew to watch the bottle while he put up the helm to bear away (*B*), then gybed (*C*), and from reaching with the wind over the starboard beam (*D*) arrived at a point where he could round up into the wind with sails flapping and the bottle just under the starboard bow. The description 'wearing ship' is given to the essential part of this manœuvre: the turn from a tack through a reach—and a gybe to the opposite tack, and for speed in turning we found it a help to ease the mainsheet in order to spill wind from the mainsail when bearing away for the gybe. I must say I'm glad that we are being drilled to a peak of efficiency in picking up a man overboard, and realise how easy it would be to lose sight of him in rough water at sea, unless one member of the crew was expressly detailed to watch him all the time.

As I look back at the next stage in our afternoon pro-
gramme I realise that it was our point of transition from
utter novices carrying out simple instructions to efficient
dinghy sailors, capable of thinking and planning under
rapidly varying weather conditions. We still have far to
go but here was our first step forward, where we've turned
all the bits of jig-saw puzzle face upwards, can recognise
each one—and have only to put them all together to have
a complete picture.

We sailed on a broad reach against the tide to a new
sailing area where the Captain pointed out a triangular
course formed by a large black Fairway buoy, a green
mooring buoy, and a paint test raft lying low in the water
(*Fig. 22*). We proceeded to sail round the triangle, leaving
all these marks to port. The total circuit could not have
been more than a quarter of a mile, but during several laps
of the course we gained really intensive practice on nearly
every point of sailing, improving steadily, and all learning
something more on each circuit, no matter who was at the
tiller, until our eventual efficiency made early efforts seem
utterly thoughtless.

We were constantly called upon to consider the effective
'set' of the sails according to wind direction on each 'leg'
of the course. We were led to calculate the effects of the
tide, to study how it could be made to work in our favour—
and though all these things fell within the range of our
experience, we had never before needed to put them to
practical use while 'making a passage'. On our very first
run from the Fairway buoy, we pointed directly to the green
buoy and were swept by the tide through an arc that was
anything but direct (Course A). We should have known
better, but we didn't think, and had to be reminded to
point our bows on a course that would leave the green buoy
several boat lengths to port, allowing for the effect of the
tide (Course B).

In rounding the green buoy we were all careful invariably
to leave it several boat lengths to port to allow for the tide,

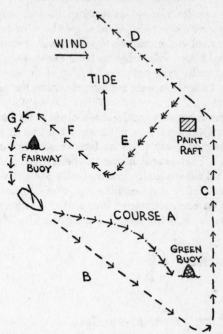

Fig. 22. Wind and tide effects on a triangular
course.

and gybed only when we were beyond it, with a direct
view of our next mark, i.e. when the raft was 'open' to us.
Then we had fast sailing on a broad reach (Course C) with
the tide under us, to the paint test raft—a dangerous looking mark that would damage our boat if we touched it.
We gave this mark a wide berth leaving it a good boat
length to port on the approach but knowing that wind and
tide would sweep us clear of it once we were round with
sheets hardened for a beat to windward (Course D) on a port
tack.   But on this course wind and tide were both against
us and we were dragged rapidly to loo'ard away from our
next mark, the Fairway buoy; at least we were on the first

circuit, but we learned by experience that as soon as we were safely round the raft we must go about to Course E, where we sailed rather slowly against wind and tide on a starboard tack but were able to hold the course with the tide under our lee bow actually helping us to keep close to the wind.   In fact we were learning to make the tide work in our favour.

On course F we soon realised we could keep quite close to 'Fairway' while passing it because both wind and tide were keeping us away from it, but we allowed ourselves more than a boat length beyond it before going about to course G and subsequently bearing away for a new circuit.

As our efficiency increased, so we reduced our time for the circuit on each successive lap, and this was especially marked as the wind freshened during the late afternoon.

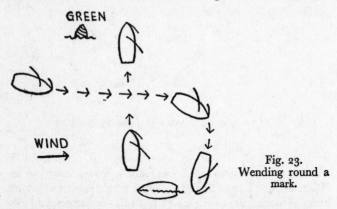

GREEN

WIND

Fig. 23.
Wending round a
mark.

With the wind across tide there were no large waves to worry us, but in the stronger wind our gybing round the green buoy developed into an operation almost too exciting for real peace of mind and so we each tried a circuit where instead of gybing at the mark we 'wended' our way round— taking a bit longer but feeling completely safe (*Fig. 23*) In 'wending' we sailed well beyond our mark for three boat lengths, then luffed up into the wind, went about to a new tack and continued our turn to a broad reach, before passing the buoy for the next leg of our course.

As the wind became even more boisterous, the Captain directed us to sail to a broad stretch of open water with no obstructions to sea room within 200 yards of us. Here we tried 'operation scared stiff'. Pretending that we were all terribly worried and didn't know what to do, we merely sat quietly in the bottom of the boat. Tiller, mainsheet and jib were all abandoned and in some trepidation we waited for dire things to happen. The sheets flapped, there was a lot of noise, but no waves washed over us, the boat remained quite steady and we realised that *Whimsy* would look after herself better if we did nothing at all, than if we took thoughtless action.

In preparation for dealing with really bad weather on some future occasion, we took the opportunity of learning something about reefing and anchoring (*Fig. 24*).

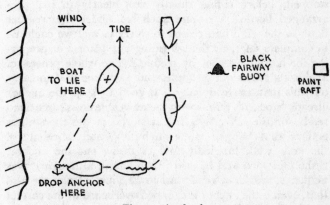

Fig. 24. Anchoring.

On the weather side of the estuary we selected a point for riding at anchor, and decided that the boat should lie fairly near the bank, directly in line with the black Fairway

D

buoy and the distant paint raft. We sailed on a broad
reach passing nearly two boat lengths to leeward of our
selected berth and while Ann dropped the jib I held
our course under mainsail only. We calculated that our
anchor rope would probably be three times the length of
the boat, and so at that distance beyond our selected berth
I luffed to forereach directly into the eye of the wind while
Tony lowered the mainsail. This was completely down
with Tony busy lashing it, as *Whimsy* ceased driving forward. Meanwhile Ann had lashed the jib, and was ready
with the anchor. As soon as our forward movement
ceased, and we began to drift back on wind and tide, Ann
lowered the anchor overboard. After paying out about a
fathom of rope she felt it light in her hand and knew the
anchor was on the bottom. As we continued to drift back
she paid out rope, almost allowing it to be dragged from
her fingers until she reached the very end, made fast to
the ring bolt, when *Whimsy* snubbed as her drifting was
stopped, before riding quietly very nearly in her pre-
arranged berth. We were anchored under the weather
bank so the wind had ceased to worry us and we could lie
in complete safety as though riding out a storm or prepar-
ing for harder weather by reefing. The whole process of
anchoring seems quite simple, and I can see that to carry
out this manœuvre quickly it is good to keep the anchor
already 'stocked', that is with the moveable cross piece fixed
ready for use. We laughed at stories of the thoughtless
actions that happen while anchoring, and especially of
the crew who, hurriedly told to throw out the anchor,
rushed forward and heaved it overboard, although it was
neither stocked nor made fast to its rope. I can see also
that, even if the anchor is dropped overboard in the correct
position with all way gone from the boat, it would be
futile to simply throw the rest of the chain or rope overboard in that spot and hope that it will sort itself out
eventually without fouling, or getting snarled up round the
fluke or the stock.

While riding at anchor we hoisted the mainsail and took a reef in it, simply by rolling the boom, to wrap round it about 18 in. of the foot of the sail, and at the same time paying out some of the main halyard, so reducing our area of canvas by about 12 square feet. I can see that reef points tied under the foot of the sail will serve a similar purpose in older craft. We hoisted our jib and our reefed main, then I hauled in the anchor rope, coiling it as it came in hand over hand. Finally when the rope was almost 'up and down' a strong tug broke out the anchor from the mud. Before stowing it aboard, I was careful to wash it clean. Meanwhile Ann controlled the jib and Tony took us on a broad reach against the tide. We sailed much more easily now that we were reefed and began to think of our return to moorings.

As we approached, we discussed our best course of action (*Fig. 25*). Course A under jib only would have been

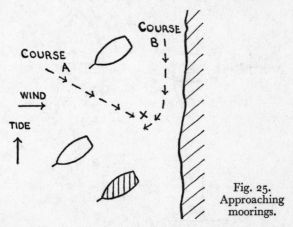

Fig. 25.
Approaching
moorings.

quite easy, but we chose course B under reefed mainsail only, and so on a broad reach we sailed against the tide, and finally eased off the sheet completely as we luffed up to our rowing boat.

Chapter 6

ARMCHAIR SESSION (1)

WHY A BOAT SAILS

WHEN a sailing boat is running with the wind astern, the wind exerts a mechanical effect in pushing the boat along. At 16–18 m.p.h., wind pressure is about 1 lb. per square foot, and if we have 100 square feet or more of canvas, set at right-angles to the wind, then we have the effect of a very powerful hand pushing the boat along (*Fig. 26, a*).

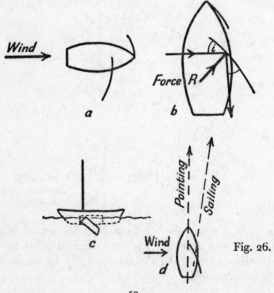

Fig. 26.

To explain the driving force of the wind when we sail
on a broad reach, mathematicians advise us that as the
wind strikes our sail at an angle (i)—the angle of incidence
of the wind—it will be deflected to leave the sail at a similar
angle, and we are assured that the 'resultant' (force R)
thrusts in a direction mid-way between these two angles,
with an effect that is something less than if the wind were
thrusting directly at right-angles. So while reaching we
have a thrust that tends to drive the boat sideways as well
as forward (b). Underneath the boat we have a centre-
plate about ½ inch thick and having a lateral area of perhaps 6 square feet (c). The centre-plate resists being
thrust broadside through the water, but it will gladly slide
edgeways through the water as the boat travels in a forward
direction. Actually while beating or reaching, a boat does
not travel directly forward on the line along which her
bows point. She drifts slightly to loo'ard because no centre-
plate has sufficient area to completely prevent sideways
drift, or leeway (d).

From experience we know our boat will sail close hauled
on a course about 45° to the wind. When we conjecture
about the force that causes the boat to move to windward,
close hauled, we find violent disagreement among the
protagonists of several theories, none of which has been
proved to the satisfaction of all.

We may be satisfied by the analogy of the orange pip
squeezed between finger and thumb. The pip is the boat.
The thumb is the wind. The resistance of the finger is like
that of our centre-plate, and so because of its shape the pip
or the boat is forced forward.

The mathematician prefers to draw a diagram as before,
but in defining the small resultant force that pushes the
boat to loo'ard and slightly forward, he so confounds us
with advanced maths, involving the sine of the angle, etc.,
that we may refuse to be convinced by something we don't
understand (Fig. 27, a).

The aeronautical expert ridicules the rest, and talks

about a 'Bernoulli effect', or the 'lift' developed by the
rigid wing of an aircraft when subjected to a forward
stream of air (*b*).   At this stage we may decide to assemble
a series of proven facts for further consideration.

We know that in a beat to windward, our sail curves

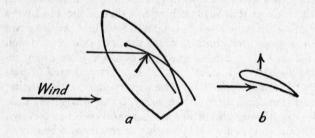

Wind

a   *b*

Fig. 27.

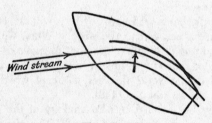

Wind stream

Fig. 28.

round into an arc (*Fig. 28*) apart from any other twisting
that may develop in the head of the sail.

We know also that it is a law of aerodynamics that when
a stream of air is deflected, its pressure is increased.   We
must recognise therefore that when the curve of our sail
deflects the main stream of air that flows along it, there is
set up a local increase of pressure on the windward side of
the sail, compared with decreased pressure to loo'ard.
It's dangerous to talk about a partial vacuum to loo'ard,

and we hesitate for a number of reasons to say that our sail is sucked forward from the loo'ard side, where pressure is less.

We may call to our aid another natural law stating that a tendency to even up pressures causes a movement to be set up from high to low pressure areas.

We may fairly logically recall also the mathematician's small resultant force acting on the windward side of the sail; and combining this with the thought of reduced pressure to loo'ard assume that our boat is pressed from the windward side of the sail in a direction slightly forward and to loo'ard. We know she resists sideways movement, and so travels forward, except for her usual leeway.

It is reasonable to assume that the jib also forms an aerofoil to give a similar effect, but we know from practical experience that our boat is nearly twice as fast with the jib as without it, in spite of its small size, and so we seek the cause of the additional drive we experience with the combined effect of jib and main.

When wind is deflected by our sail, the stream of air passing on the longer course to loo'ard must travel more swiftly than the air deflected on the windward side. Further, as there seems to be increased movement of air at any time between two buildings, or through an alley-way, we may expect some increase of normal air speed in the space or slot between jib and mainsail.

When the two factors are combined it seems that the normal action of the jib is considerably exaggerated by the 'slot effect' between the two sails.

This is by no means the complete story and much experimental work is being done concerning the imperviousness and surface friction of the material of the sail itself. Cotton sail-cloth, wax-treated cotton, and synthetic materials like nylon and Orlon are showing widely different results, and it seems that only by trial and error can we gain practical knowledge to support or destroy our various theories.

The shape of her sails has a profound effect on the

performance of a boat. A sail of the Bermudian type with a high aspect ratio (a very tall mast in relation to the length of the boom) has a long leading edge or luff to the sail, along which the aerodynamic effect may work (*Fig. 29, a*). The luff, or leading edge, is shorter on a gaff rigged

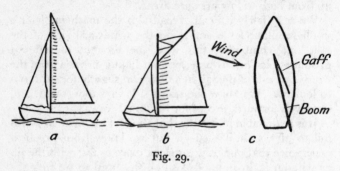

Fig. 29.

mainsail (a quadrangular sail hung from a spar called the gaff) and consequently the aerodynamic force is less in close hauled sailing (*b*).

Note also that on a beat to windward, the gaff, supported by the peak halyard, will sag away to loo'ard—so losing some efficiency—by spilling wind (*c*).

Concerning sail plans we can say with some certainty that the gaff rig can be as effective as Bermudian for running, when thrust depends on canvas area, but for beating close hauled to windward, the Bermudian is more effective.

When the wind flows over a sail, the mast ruffles the smooth flow of the air-stream and mast-eddies caused near the luff of a Bermudian mainsail will considerably lower its efficiency. No matter how we streamline the mast, the eddy effect persists. A jib set on a wire stay doesn't suffer in this way from eddies, and so, area for area, it is generally more efficient than a mainsail. While we used to favour a jib in the form of a low triangle, it seems that we should get increased aerodynamic force by using a taller jib, with its longer luff, and its halyard carried higher towards the mast-head (*Fig. 30*).

Here then are reasons why in modern craft there is a tendency to use jibs of ever increasing size—and where the

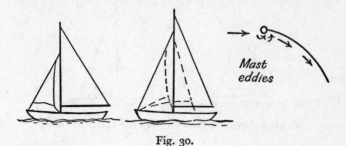

Fig. 30.

jib considerably overlaps the luff of the mainsail we have the additional advantage of greater 'slot effect' between the two sails.

In his search for the most effective sail plan under all conditions, the designer uses a mainsail of high aspect ratio —tall mast and short boom—in conjunction with a tall, overlapping jib. Caught suddenly in a storm, the skipper of such a craft merely takes down the very large jib—and bends on a smaller one, reducing his area of canvas but keeping much of his power to beat to windward.

SAIL PLANS

Our simplest little sailing boat has a single mainsail carried on a mast that is stepped well forward. The sail is hung from a gaff, and typical craft of this type are scows (*Fig. 31, a*). Where a tall Bermudian type of single sail is used we have much more effective sailing, and such a type is clearly shown in the Finn—one of the Olympic classes (*b*).

A boat carrying two sails is called a sloop and sails are known as the main and the jib. We can have a gaff rigged sloop (*Fig. 32, a*), a gunter gaff sloop (*b*), where the gaff is carried by a wire in a vertical position above the mast, or we can have a Bermudian sloop (*c*) with the tall rig already mentioned.

When boats were very heavily built, needing a lot of

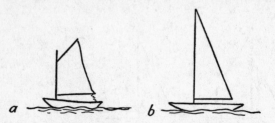

Fig. 31. *a.* Lugger and scow.   *b.* Finn and Y.W. Solo.

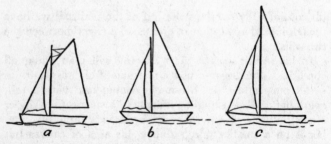

Fig. 32. *a.* Gaff sloop.   *b.* Gunter gaff.   *c.* Bermudian sloop.

driving power, the sail plan overlapped the boat and the gaff-rigged cutter (*Fig. 33, a*) was a familiar sight. Here the jib was carried from a bowsprit, the foresail was in the normal triangle between the stemhead and the mast, and the gaff mainsail had a very long boom which overhung the stern of the boat. A modern cutter (*b*) has all her rigging inboard and uses a Bermudian mainsail.

Those enthusiasts who are very fond of single-handed sailing often prefer to have more sails where each one is small enough to be easily handled without mechanical aid,

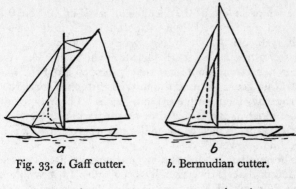

Fig. 33. *a*. Gaff cutter.   *b*. Bermudian cutter.

Fig. 34. *a*. Gaff-rigged yawl.   *b*. Gaff-rigged ketch.

Wishbone

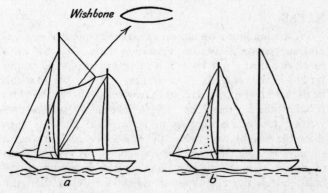

Fig. 35. *a*. Wishbone ketch.   *b*. Schooner.

rather than have sails that are few in number, but large in size, and requiring winches to operate halyards and sheets. Such craft are the yawl (*Fig. 34, a*) and ketch (*b*), each carrying a mizzen—a small sail aft of the main. The yawl carries her mizzen on a mast that is stepped aft of the tiller or steering gear. Where the mizzen is stepped forward of the steering, then we recognise a ketch. These types are encountered in the larger sizes needing winches for sheets and halyards, as well as in small craft where all work is by direct man-power.

A Bermudian ketch has a large triangular area between the masts that is not usefully occupied. In a wishbone ketch (*Fig. 35, a*) this area is filled by two sails. The 'main' has its widest part aloft and is controlled by a twin boom (a wishbone-shaped spar) with its main sheet passing through a block at the head of the mizzen mast. The second sail is a triangle, set on a stay that runs from the lower part of the mainmast to the top of the mizzen. The boom of this sail is connected to the mainmast in the normal way.

Occasionally we see a schooner (*b*), a craft with two masts, but with the taller mast stepped aft.

KEELS

We are familiar with our own iron centre-plate (*Fig. 36, a*) and appreciate its use in preventing undue 'leeway' on a reach or a beat. We know it is carried in its long rectangular box in the centre of the boat, and that it pivots on a bolt at the fore end of the box, so that when we lower the plate it hangs down 3 or 4 feet under our keel. As well as preventing too much sagging to leeward, it provides considerable weight well below the water line and this extra stability is valuable while we are sailing. A simpler form of plate known as a dagger-plate (*b*) is often used on small craft, but is more difficult to adjust for depth than the normal centre-plate. A sailing barge with its flat bottom has neither centre-plate nor dagger-plate, and thus the inside of the boat provides a large area of cargo space. The barge is prevented from sagging to leeward when she is sailing by having a leeboard to lower over either side, which ever side is to loo'ard (c).

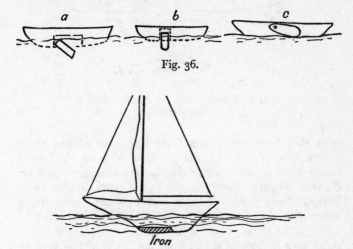

Fig. 36.

Fig. 37. A keel boat.

Most cruisers and larger racing craft have a fixed keel (*Fig. 37*), which has the further purpose of putting the maximum amount of weight well below the centre of buoyancy of the boat, but more of this later. The great disadvantage of a keel boat sailing in an estuary is that when she runs aground on a falling tide she cannot pull up her plate and sail away again, but must generally remain on the mud until the tide refloats her.

SHEER

A boat viewed from the side gives an impression of good looks or indifferent appearance, chiefly by the curve of her 'sheer', which is the line of the deck running from bow to stern. Working boats, fishermen and the like, generally have a bold sheer (*Fig. 38, a*) with high bows designed to keep the boat dry under working conditions in a sea-way,

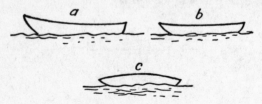

Fig. 38. *a*. Bold sheer. *b*. Normal sheer.
c. Reverse sheer.

with the sheer line falling from the bows to amidships before levelling to the stern. It may even rise again towards the stern. Where the line is not exaggerated we speak of 'normal' sheer (*b*). In recent years designers and builders have produced boats with very low bows and a sheer that rises to a high point amidships before falling away to the stern. This is known as reverse sheer (*c*), or sometimes as hogged sheer, from the shape of the 'hog' or keel which often takes such a curve under the boat. Reverse sheer represents progress in design that may not be beautiful to conservative eyes—and most sailors are essentially conservative at heart—but it does save weight and constructional expense at the bows, while providing height amidships where it is most needed for cabin space.

STEM, STERN, OVERHANGS

Many boats have the same 'length waterline' as 'length overall' (*Fig. 39, a*). They have a straight (vertical) stem or bow and a vertical stern. Other craft have a long overhang above the waterline at both stem and stern (*b*). Such construction has a definite purpose which is discussed on page 90. The stern may have the same shape as the bow, to give a double ended boat of the life-boat type or, with slight variations, the Norwegian and canoe type. On other craft, the stern takes the form of a broad transom as though a long boat had been cut off some way aft of

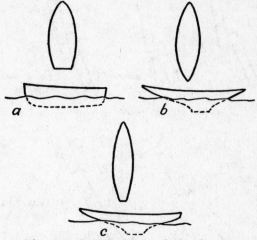

Fig. 39. *a*. Straight stem.   *b*. Overhangs.
c. Counter stern.

amidships and the broad gap filled in. Often where we have an overhanging stern we have a small tucked up counter (*c*), that gives all the benefits of an overhang without unduly increasing length by being carried to a point.

CONSTRUCTION

There are a very large variety of possible ways in which a boat can be built. She may be of a sea-water resisting aluminium alloy or even of steel, but generally she is built of wood. Where the long planks that run fore and aft on the side of the boat are overlapped, we describe the construction as 'clinker' (*Fig. 40*). When this method is used, the edge of the lower plank is 'faired' away to give a broad area of contact at the overlap.

In 'carvel' building (*Fig. 41*) the edges of the planks are

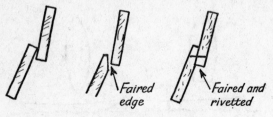

Fig. 40. Clinker building.

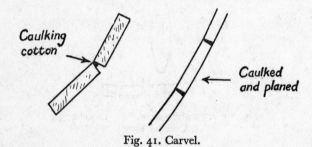

Fig. 41. Carvel.

butted together—the space between is rammed tight with caulking cotton, the final space filled with putty or a compound that doesn't harden completely for at least the first season, then the whole of the side of the boat is planed to give a smooth surface. When this is well painted hardly a joint will be visible.

In clinker and carvel construction we gain maximum strength if each plank runs the full length from stem to stern, and so each plank for the boat is cut from a large plank that is really a 'slice' taken from the original log. There is considerable waste because each of these planks must be cut to its own particular curve before it can be fitted (*Fig. 42*). If we cut our original plank into long strips about an inch wide, then these can be fitted one on top of the other to form the side of the boat. They are pliable enough to take the curve that has been designed,

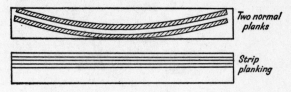

Two normal planks

Strip planking

Fig. 42.

and when they are nailed and glued together, form a very sound job of construction. This is known as strip planking, and completely avoids waste of timber.

It is generally cheaper to buy timber from short logs than from long ones. If we can go to a little more trouble in building with short planks, the saving on planking will be offset by increased labour costs, but we can have a diagonal built craft where the planks run from the gunwale down to the keel, and if we have double diagonal planking with a layer of canvas between, then we have a really water-tight boat that is very strongly made (*Fig. 43*).

Fig. 43.

Boats are expensive chiefly because of labour costs, but when a means was found to reduce costs by using water-proof plywood, it was the amateur builder rather than the professional who derived most benefit. If a hard chine boat is designed—with angled bilges rather than a round cross section (*Fig. 44*)—then a 14-foot boat can be built with only eight sections of plywood. This is the method that attracts the amateur, and several firms now specialise in making things even easier for him by producing kits of parts for home building. A set of frames is supplied, and these are returnable to the firm when the boat is completed.

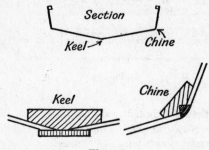

Fig. 44.

If the amateur builder takes care in first setting up his frames or moulds, then, provided he can use a screwdriver, a plane, a rabbet plane, a chisel and lots of sandpaper, he can build his own boat.

The designer has ensured that the materials to be used will not need to be unduly bent or twisted (certainly not more than can be effected with a kettle of boiling water), while the special glues that are recommended even make the use of screws almost unnecessary.

The amateur builder quite definitely need not be a skilled craftsman. He must have unlimited patience, he must never be in a hurry, and he must be prepared to 'fit and adjust' *ad infinitum*—taking his job as a pleasure rather than a money-saving task.

In very recent years, plastic and fibre-glass hulls have become increasingly popular. They are built on a mould from which the shell of the boat is subsequently lifted. If literally hundreds of people could decide to have the one class of boat, then moulded hulls of that particular class could probably be made very cheaply, but it will be appreciated that this method is expensive, if only one boat is to be made from a particular mould.

The catamaran at its simplest, a platform resting on twin hulls, must be regarded as a class on its own. While the design is probably one of the oldest in the world, modern versions provide incredibly fast sailing, combined with almost uncanny stability. Because twin hulls rarely turn so readily as a single hull, few catamarans are 'lively' in going about, and 'slow in stays' is the common criticism.

Where the twin hulls are of identical and symmetrical construction, i.e. both shaped like canoes, then a dagger-plate is used to prevent undue leeway (*Fig. 45, a*).

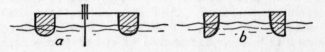

Fig. 45. *a*. Symmetrical hulls.   *b*. Assymmetrical hulls.

Asymmetrical hulls (*b*), presenting a near-vertical face to loo'ard on any point of sailing—can offer enough lateral resistance to obviate the need for a dagger-plate.

The difficulty of fitting a single rudder, that would have to work in the disturbed water between the hulls, has led designers of both versions to adopt small twin rudders, one for each hull, but operated as a linked unit.

When all the variables of boat design and construction are considered, different sail plans, hull shapes and keels, it is easy to see why outside the normal 'classes', we so rarely find two boats exactly alike—and why the beginner is rather bewildered in making a choice.

Chapter 7

FIFTH SAILING SESSION

HERE was our most eventful day—a day of achievement—
a major land-mark in our progress. The wind was fresh
from our side of the estuary in the morning and as we prepared for sailing we rolled a reef in the mainsail. The
problem 'to reef or not to reef' seems easily solved by
logical thought. If the wind remains just as fresh as it is,
we, as beginners, have as much driving power as we need
with a reefed mainsail. If it freshens still more, we won't
need to worry unduly, while if the wind should fall away,
then it's a very simple matter to luff up and shake out the
reef. As the Captain says, 'Carrying a couple of rolls in
the main may stamp us as novices, but that's better than

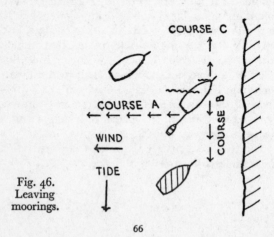

Fig. 46.
Leaving
moorings.

being cursed as fools for carrying more canvas than we can manage.'

For this session we made fast our rowing dinghy astern of *Whimsy*, and then considered how to leave moorings (*Fig. 46*). We felt sure that under jib only we could sail away on course A or on course B. Under main and jib we could select course B or C. As we proposed towing the rowing dinghy we chose course C. The jib was backed to starboard for a moment to turn our bows still more to port, when we hardened sheets and sailed off on a reach against the tide, with the dinghy astern in no danger of being caught against any other boat.

On reaching open water we spent some time on a brief revision of precautions against collision, five simple points that we had been putting into practice during the last two days, but on which we were now tested. Actually we studied these as homework last night and knew them by heart.

1. TAKE AVOIDING ACTION EARLY TO GIVE THE OTHER SKIPPER A CLEAR INDICATION OF YOUR INTENTION.

2. IF YOU ARE SAILING FREE, THEN GIVE WAY TO A BOAT CLOSE HAULED (*Fig. 47*). White boat will give way,

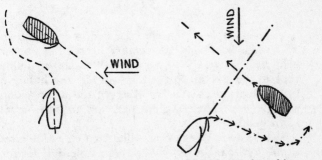

Fig. 47.   Fig. 48. 'Starboard.'

by putting up her helm, bearing away, and going under stern of black boat.

3. IF YOU ARE CLOSE HAULED ON THE PORT TACK (wind coming over the port bow) THEN GIVE WAY TO A BOAT CLOSE HAULED ON A STARBOARD TACK (*Fig. 48*).

White boat will keep clear by bearing away to pass astern of shaded boat, before resuming her close hauled course again.

4. IF BOTH BOATS ARE SAILING FREE AND YOU HAVE THE WIND OVER YOUR PORT BEAM, THEN GIVE WAY (*Fig. 49*).

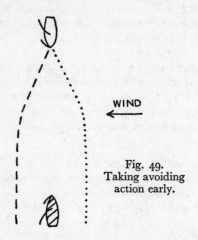

WIND

Fig. 49.
Taking avoiding
action early.

A clear example of the need for taking early action. The white boat may alter course by putting up her helm to bear away—giving the other skipper ample time to make a similar gesture—in his case luffing a little to indicate that he has observed and taken action accordingly. The two ships pass port to port—or at night 'red to red'.

Should the skipper of the white boat choose to alter course by luffing a little—allowing ample time for the other skipper to observe and take action, then the two boats will pass starboard to starboard—or at night 'green to green'.

5. IN OVERTAKING A BOAT AHEAD, you are free to pass under her lee or several boat lengths to windward, but it is most discourteous to pass *CLOSE* to windward of a boat ahead, giving her your 'dirty' wind—the turbulent air stream that your passing creates (*Fig. 50*).

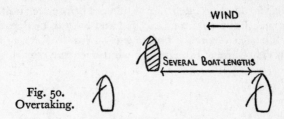

WIND

SEVERAL BOAT-LENGTHS

Fig. 50.
Overtaking.

We each knew the correct thing to do after due thought, but between us we managed to give quick answers to all imaginary situations presented to us. As a means of 'putting on the brake' while an imaginary boat passed in front of us, we practised luffing up to hold a position 'in stays'—pointing directly into the wind with sails flapping, before going about or bearing away—while retaining enough momentum to turn. Occasionally we misjudged this, and put *Whimsy* 'in irons', heading into the wind, but without any forward movement. Then we tried to keep her bows pointing in the same direction while we were drifted astern by wind and tide—'making a sternboard'. By backing the jib we could resume our old course or turn to a new one, as we wished.

We had already learned that, while we could normally expect every courtesy from power craft, we must keep clear of those working boats obliged by reason of their greater draught to follow the deep water channel of the estuary, and we were reminded again that it's really dangerous for a sailing boat to tack across the bows of a motor boat, in the fond belief that her skipper will anticipate this very move.

I was aware that all this final revision was in fact the

prelude to our sailing alone, and as we reached our triangular course of yesterday the Captain prepared to leave us. He proposed to anchor the rowing boat at our gybing point on the triangle.

After giving each a special point to remember, he pulled the rowing boat alongside, untied the painter, stepped aboard and was gone from us, almost before we could feel worried, but we were too excited and busy to be dismayed. At the tiller I checked our course—a run to Fairway buoy that should have brought the wind over our port quarter.

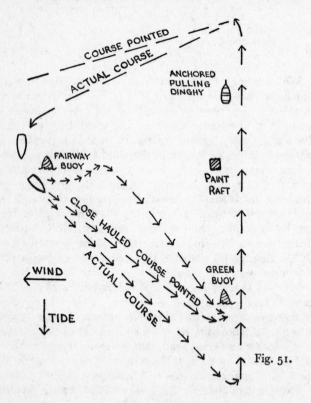

Fig. 51.

Allowing for the effect of the tide, however, I pointed a course that would leave 'Fairway' well to port, and actually sailed with the wind almost dead astern. We rounded the mark with two boat lengths to spare—good for my peace of mind—and hauled in the sheets for our beat on a port tack from Fairway to the green buoy (*Fig. 51*).

On this leg the powerful effect of the tide was really driven home for us. We held port tack as directed to a point where we could see the rowing boat open of the green buoy before going about, but by then we had been swept several lengths off course. A broad reach against the tide with the wind over the starboard beam carried us steadily to the green buoy, on past the paint raft—no longer a mark on our new course—and soon we were up to the Captain in his anchored rowing boat. We sailed well beyond him, allowing two boat lengths to avoid his anchor rope and then a third length to allow for the effect of the tide, before gybing round to sail the triangle again. On subsequent circuits we held course for 'Fairway' as before, but beyond the mark went about to a starboard tack and held this until we judged it easy to just clear the green buoy on port. Then after tacking again round the mark we could bear away for the reach to the anchored rowing boat.

As we took turns at the tiller, I felt inordinately pleased to think that we had all made such rapid progress, though it must be admitted that we were essentially a democratic crew. There wasn't exactly a committee meeting to decide policy, but the helmsman would generally say, 'Do you think this is the time to go about?'—and when the eventual 'order' came, it was really a result of general agreement. We were thinking aloud—pooling ideas—and were completely absorbed in our sailing.

Eventually we picked up the Captain again. Approaching on a broad reach under mainsail only we spilled wind until we were merely holding our position against the tide with the rowing boat under our starboard bow clear of sails and boom (*Fig. 52*). The Captain had his anchor rope 'up and down' and, as we took his painter, he hauled in his anchor and moved right aft in the rowing boat while we hoisted our jib, hardened our sheets and sailed for moorings with the rowing boat in tow. I understand that if the

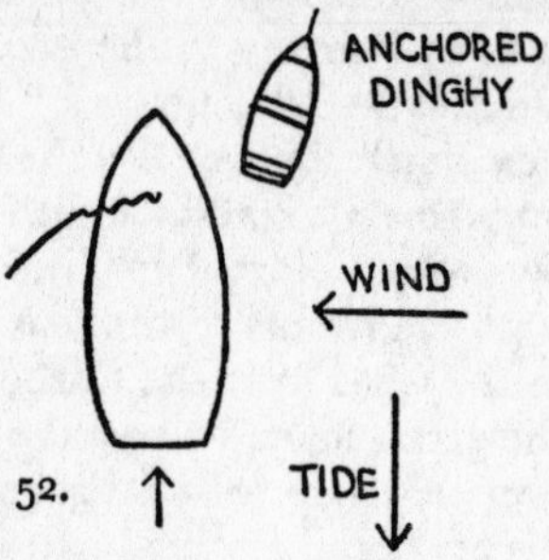

Fig. 52.

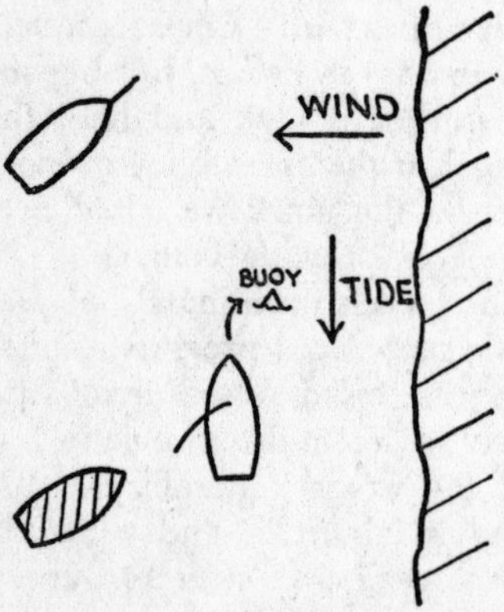

Fig. 53.

Captain had sat amidships or in the bows of the rowing boat, it would have 'sheered' about from side to side following a zigzag course behind us.

As we neared the anchorage we discussed means of pick-ing up our mooring. On casting off the rowing boat, we lowered the jib and sailed on a broad reach against the tide under mainsail only before luffing up into the wind with the mooring buoy under our starboard bow (*Fig. 53*). The Captain brought the rowing boat alongside, watched while we left everything ship-shape aboard, and we all came ashore feeling very elated by our achievement, and quite ready to sail completely alone in the afternoon.

Chapter 8

KNOTS IN USE ABOARD

I BEGIN to appreciate that when you learn to sail, you must also achieve patience. In the afternoon, the wind fell so light we realised it was quite impossible to manœuvre our boat against the tide, and there was nothing we could do about it. We were assured that 'The wind will certainly blow again—sometime', and so we went aboard—all quietly whistling for a wind, to revise or learn every knot and splice that we are likely to need in the immediate future. By now we can all make the figure of eight knot (*Fig. 54, a*) for the end of the jib sheet and know from

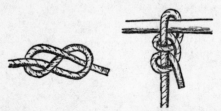

Fig. 54. *a*. Figure of eight. *b*. Two half hitches.

experience that this is easily undone after a day's sailing no matter how wet it may be or how tightly it has been pulled. We can tie two half hitches (*b*) for making fast our mooring rope to the ring bolt in the bows, and for making fast the dinghy when we go ashore.

A clove hitch (*Fig. 55*) for making fast the dinghy painter to the heavy mooring rope, is very simple and we have even practised this knot with one hand, while standing on the

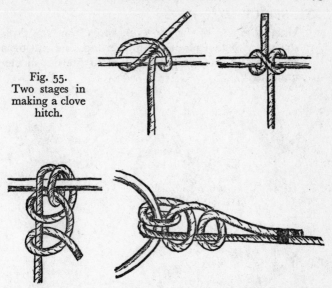

Fig. 55.
Two stages in
making a clove
hitch.

Fig. 56. *a*. Fisherman's bend. *b*. Fisherman's bend with seizing.

iron ladder let into the wall of the quayside, to make fast our dinghy to one of the rungs.

The anchor rope on *Whimsy* is tied with a fisherman's bend (*Fig. 56, a*)—and we practised this until we could make it reasonably quickly, then finally we added a seizing of whipping cotton (*b*).

At the end of each sheet and halyard we found an eye splice round a thimble—a metal former, curved to hold the rope and provide an 'eye' that is always open—as a protection from wear. This eye splice seemed rather complicated, but within an hour we could all manage it, and found the several stages easy to remember. We practised on 4-foot lengths of hambro line or cod line, and now have spare lashings aboard, each with an eye splice at one end, and a back splice at the other.

EYE SPLICE (*Fig. 57*)

1. Unlay the end of the rope (*a*), spread out the three strands with the middle strand on top, and put on a short stopping of whipping cotton to prevent further unlaying.

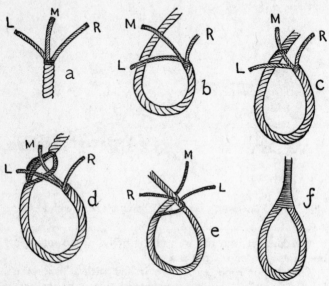

Fig. 57. Eye splice.

2. Bend the end of the rope, into a loop or 'bight' in which the thimble will be enclosed, allowing middle and left strands to pass across the main rope (*b*).

3. With a marline spike, make a space under a strand of the standing part of the rope, and tuck the middle strand through this space—working from right to left (c).

4. Tuck the left-hand end under the strand beyond the first tuck—still from right to left (*d*).

5. Now turn the rope over and tuck the final strand—the

locking strand—again from right to left (*e*). At this stage a loop is formed, that should grip the thimble when all three end strands are pulled tight.

6. Each end strand is then crossed over one strand in the main rope and tucked under the next, until each has been given a total of three tucks.

7. The strands may now be halved in thickness by cutting away before being tucked twice more, to give the splice a taper.

8. If the splice is rolled between the sole of the plimsoll and the deck the tucks are evened into a smooth splice.

9. Finally the splice may be served with whipping cotton (*f*).

BACK SPLICE (*Fig. 58*)

1. A short stopping is tied round the rope about 3 inches from the end, then the strands are opened to the stopping and spread wide apart (*a*).

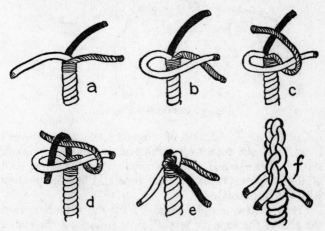

Fig. 58. Back splice.

2. Strand left is placed over strand right (*b*).

3. Strand right is bent over left to enclose it and is then placed across middle strand (*c*).

4. Middle strand is bent round right to enclose it and is then passed down through the bight first formed in strand left (*d*).

5. All strands are pulled tightly together to make a crown knot—with the three end strands all pointing back along the main piece of rope.

6. Each end strand is passed over one strand in the main rope and tucked under the next strand. When three tucks have been completed, the ends are cut off and the back splice is rolled under the foot.

We renewed the whipping at the end of the sheets, and found that with waxed twine we quickly learned to make a really neat and effective job, using the method known as 'common' whipping (*Fig. 59*).

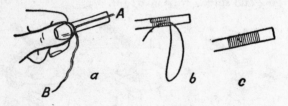

Fig. 59. Common whipping.

Cut off a 3-foot length of whipping twine. In the left hand, hold the rope to be whipped, leaving only two or three inches exposed. Lay a couple of inches of one end of the whipping twine over the rope and lock in position with the thumb (*a*).

Wrap the twine tightly round from the thumb toward the end of the rope for several turns so locking the end A of the whipping twine. Now place the end B of the whipping twine along the end of the rope in the opposite direction to A and continue to make several more turns,

their different ways. On this side of the Atlantic we favoured narrow boats, introduced outside ballast for great stability, and reached the typical English design of the long, narrow boat, with deep ballast keel—the 'plank on edge' type (*Fig. 63*).

With the weight of the ballast so far below the centre of buoyancy it exerted a very powerful leverage in counteracting the heeling action caused by pressure of wind on the sails. The boat was virtually uncapsizeable, because the more she heeled the more the weight of the ballast tended to exert a strong righting effect, while at a marked angle of heel there was more 'spilling of wind' from the sails than when the mast was vertical. These factors are of vital importance in all keel boats.

On the other side of the Atlantic, designers preferred beamy boats with shallow draught, generally with centreplates, and relied on the beam of the boat more than on ballast for stability. These trends persist.

Meanwhile, in this country, at least one designer was attacking his problems scientifically, and Froude carried out tank tests in which he towed models of different boats through water at varying speeds in order to measure their 'resistance'. He was able to say quite definitely that when a boat moves through the water, the resistance that it meets is due to friction and to the shape of the boat. At low speeds, skin friction—the normal friction between the hull surface and the water—accounts for most of the resis-

Fig. 64.

tance that occurs. At higher speeds the shape or form of the boat is much more important, and a bluff-bowed hull lying deep in the water causes very much more resistance than a slim, shallow-draught canoe-shaped hull. Subsequently, Bental built the craft *Jullinar*. Her bow and stern were rigorously cut away below the waterline in order to give a smaller area of wetted surface (*Fig. 64*). In spite of dire forebodings by critics of the day, this boat was very fast, and did not drown her crew.

Designers and builders of boats have generally allowed adequate width in the stern to provide space for helmsman and crew. As a result of her fuller sections aft, the stern of the boat was more buoyant than her bows, and with two or three people in a cockpit aft, she would not sink more than an inch or two below her normal water line. Such a design carried certain penalties.

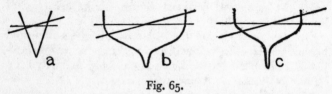

Fig. 65.

Fig. 65 shows cross sections of a boat: near the bows (*a*); amidships (*b*); and near the stern (*c*). If we consider the section amidships we can expect that when the boat heels, she lifts a certain amount of her side planking out of the water to windward, and on the opposite side, to loo'ard, immerses an equal amount. The same should apply for'ard, and aft. From the diagram (*a*) representing the bows, note the very small amount of boat buried in the water when she heels compared with the amount at the stern (*c*). Yet our boat is more or less rigid and we cannot change her buoyancy. Rather than immerse such a large amount of boat aft where she is especially buoyant, compared with for'ard, the boat evens up the immersed volumes fore and aft, i.e. she alters her trim fore and aft when she heels, by dipping her bows much more than shown in the diagram. In fact she 'roots' when driven hard, and in the extreme case such a boat will ride her bows under if she carries enough canvas.

It is now normal practice to use a hull of 'symmetrical' design, to give a 'balanced' boat. Modern craft therefore are generally 'filled out' for'ard to give rounded bows that are more buoyant, while aft, the hull, at least below the waterline, has a similar shape. To provide cockpit space the sections aft are made broader only some distance above the waterline.

We owe much to model yachtsmen, who in their experiments leading to a design able to beat to windward with the tiller locked amidships, have made a real contribution to knowledge of hull and sail balance.

Fig. 65*a*. Hollow masts. The two drawings on the left show first and second stages of the same mast.

Early in this century experiments with the 'marconi' mast—scorned because of its maze of rigging—paved the way for the Bermudian rig, with mast track, and hollow spars of timber or aluminium alloy. The hollow wooden mast may be made from two pieces of timber hollowed and glued together, or may be built up in box section.

In quite recent years designers have given yachts considerably more free-board and this carries two very real advantages. The boat can heel a little farther before waves are running over the deck, and—even more important—free-board increased by a few inches provides the extra headroom that vastly improves comfort in the cabin.

The modern yachtsman, then, has the experience of generations of designers and builders to guide him in his choice of boat, whether it be a cruiser, or a racing craft with slim, canoe-shaped body, appendage keel, and rudder carried on a skeg, such as in *Fig. 66*.

Boats are often compared with women, and certainly the different combinations of physical characteristics in each case provide infinite variety, but in the case of a boat, her physical qualities—length, beam, draught, weight, sail plan—directly affect her virtues of speed, comfort and

Fig. 66.

safety. Her designer can ensure that any one, or possibly two, of these virtues are of the highest possible order—and as a result the third will be partly sacrificed. Design involves compromise. A yacht designed solely for speed will provide little comfort aboard, while one planned to give her owner the maximum of comfortable accommodation in the cockpit and saloon cannot also be extremely fast.

Consider the simplest means of designing for speed (*Fig. 67*). When young Ann sits in the rowing dinghy and

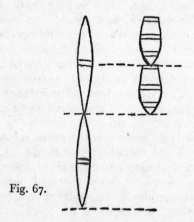

Fig. 67.

gives one strong pull to drive the boat forward its own length through the water, then in effect, if the laden dinghy weighs 3 cwt., i.e. displaces that weight of water, Ann's effort has caused the boat to push aside about 3 cwt. of water in moving forward for one length. In seeking speed we can design a rowing dinghy twice as long and half as wide, with exactly the same laden weight. A similar effort by Ann should again drive the boat forward its own length in pushing aside the same displacement of water. But the boat has travelled twice as far. Although this double distance may not have been covered in the same period of time, obviously here is a means of designing a boat faster than the beamy little tub we normally row.

The factors linking speed, safety and comfort may be illustrated if we examine the behaviour of different types of craft. First consider a barrel floating in the water. It rolls (capsizes) very easily, but if two barrels are lashed together side by side, then they are extremely difficult to turn over. A normal broad-beamed sailing dinghy has a bottom in the shape of two barrels—she has round bilges— and on a waterline length of 16 ft. has a beam of about 6 ft. With the addition of an iron centre-plate, she forms a stable boat and weighs about 5 cwt. unladen. On the wind, she heels only slightly and her crew may sit in comfort aboard her (*Fig. 68, a*).

A boat just as long, having less beam but again with an iron centre-plate, will be lighter, she will displace a smaller weight of water, and we can expect her to be appreciably faster. She will heel more readily and instead of sitting inboard, the crew must balance the boat by 'sitting out' (*b*).

Next we can select the Hornet, a boat of 16 ft. length, built of waterproof plywood, and having a wooden centre-plate to reduce total weight to just over 2 cwt. She has so little 'built in' stability that, while afloat in quiet water without sails, if helmsman and crew both leaned over one side together to retrieve a tiller that had fallen overboard they would probably join it in the water. The boat needs

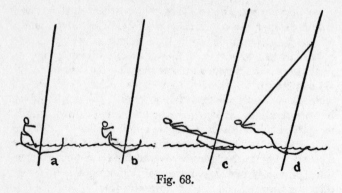

Fig. 68.

balancing at all times—and both helmsman and crew must act as moving ballast while sailing. To make the crew's weight more effective, he or she 'sits out' on a plank that slides to windward on either side. The boat is incredibly fast, and though her planing hull (see p. 90) aids her speed, she forms an excellent example for our illustration (c).

To balance a '505', the crew stand on the side of the boat and lie in space over the water, supported by a 'trapeze', fixed at a point high on the mast and clipped to a chest harness (d).

In the last two cases, our search for speed as the all-important virtue produces satisfying results, and for about £150 we can buy a boat as fast as a Dragon that would cost many times that figure initially, and be correspondingly expensive in maintenance costs.

But what of the other virtues—comfort and safety?

The modern Hornet has an extremely high safety factor (Fig. 69). The bow section forward of the mast is completely enclosed by a bulkhead, to form a watertight compartment. Side-decks run from the gunwale to the top of the centre-board box to provide two more 'buoyancy' chambers. The rest of the boat aft has a 'deck' just above the normal waterline level of the boat, and a hole as big as a bucket may be cut in the stern. When waves or spray wash over the boat, all water runs out through the centre-board box or swills over the helmsman's 'deck', and escapes through the hole in the transom.   The boat has so much built-in buoyancy that she cannot sink, and when two class

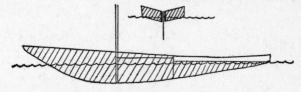

Fig. 69. Built-in buoyancy.

rules are added (*a*) skipper and crew must carry life-jackets, and (*b*) the helmsman cannot finish a race without his crew, then we have the highest possible factors of speed and safety that can be found in a class racing boat.   Cap-sizing is recognised as a normal occurrence in racing, but by standing on the centre-plate the helmsman rights the boat in a matter of seconds and can carry out this man-œuvre without getting wet above his knees.   The crew must be prepared to wade knee deep in water while helping to launch the boat, sit on the plank in a cloud of spray throughout the race, take capsizing as part of the game, then jump overboard in shallow water to steady the boat as she returns to the slipway at the end of the race.   It isn't comfortable, and so the family party, especially with a timid parent, must sacrifice speed to enjoy the greater comfort of the beamy boat.

The speed of a fixed-keel boat is very closely related to her length, and a speed-length ratio may be given as

$$\frac{\text{Speed in Knots}}{\sqrt{\text{Length of the load waterline in feet}}}$$

A well-designed boat beating close hauled to windward can achieve a ratio of as much as 0·8.   Running with the wind astern she will be considerably faster and may increase the ratio to 1·5. An example illustrates this fairly clearly.

Boats of 16 ft. and 25 ft. on the water line and beating to windward present ratios:

$$\frac{\text{Knots}}{\sqrt{16}} = 0\cdot8; \qquad \frac{\text{Knots}}{4} = 0\cdot8; \qquad \therefore \text{Knots} = 3\cdot2$$

$$\frac{\text{Knots}}{\sqrt{25}} = 0\cdot8; \qquad \frac{\text{Knots}}{5} = 0\cdot8; \qquad \therefore \text{Knots} = 4$$

Similarly with the wind aft, our 16-footer may reach a speed of 6 knots, and the 25-footer a speed of 7·5 knots.

We know that as a boat nears her maximum speed, form resistance—due to her shape—has more effect in preventing a further increase of speed than has friction resistance. The beamy cruiser, lying fairly deep in the water, will not achieve the same speed as the modern racing hull, with a canoe-shaped body and appendage keel.

As the speed of a boat increases, so the form wave she creates builds up to a high point near her bows and another well aft. If the boat is towed through the water at a speed much in excess of her normal maximum, then the form wave created will completely inundate the boat.

A craft having a waterline length of 25 ft. with overhangs fore and aft giving her perhaps 31 ft. total length, will benefit by the greater effective length when she travels at speed. Her buoyant ends will support her on a longer waterline and she will attain a higher maximum speed, than a boat of 25 ft. overall (*Fig. 70*).

Modern dinghies obviously do not obey the speed-length ratios already quoted. Designers in recent years have improved hull shape to the point where the boat develops hydrodynamic lift as it is driven through the water and the 'planing' dinghy is seen with her 'bow' wave nearly as far aft as the side stays (*Fig. 71*).

Sail area needs to be at least twice the wetted surface area to give adequate driving power, but this is effective in making the boat plane only if the hull is light enough to be lifted, and has a shape that encourages hydrodynamic lift.

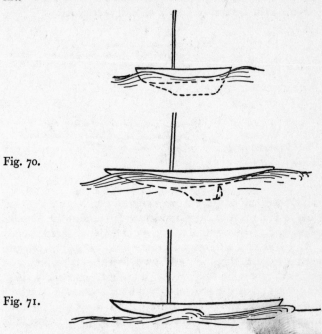

Fig. 70.

Fig. 71.

In *Fig. 72* the two hulls *a* and *b*, offer resistance as they are driven through the water. If we regard the water as moving forward to meet the hull, we can more easily note its effect. In *a* the hull offers direct resistance. In *b* the force of the water against an inclined area will cause resistance with an upward component that tends to 'lift' the bow into a planing position.

The weight factor is obviously of vital importance. The plywood or moulded hull is light enough to 'lift', yet is

designed to have an adequate area of wetted surface amidships and aft on which to plane, even when the bows of the
boat are lifted well above water level.

Planing hulls, then, are capable of speeds far in excess
of craft of equal length, with deep ballast keels, and they
provide exhilarating racing of the highest order.

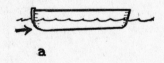

a

Fig. 72.
Hydrodynamic
lift.

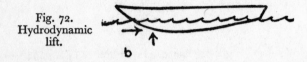

b

The skipper and crew are generally young enough—at
least in outlook—to enjoy moderate discomfort for the sake
of really fast sailing in a boat they can easily afford.

Literally tens of thousands of enthusiasts enjoy week-end
racing in class dinghies, and trail their boats to area and
national championships. As a result, extremely high
standards of sailing prevail throughout these classes, which
range in size, speed and price—from the Cadet, a little
over 10 ft. in length, costing about £75, and specially
designed for junior helmsman and crew.

At the upper end of the scale we can include the 'Flying
Dutchman', built of laminated wood veneers, bonded with
plastic, having an overall length of nearly 20 ft., and
reputed to be capable of speeds of over 14 knots. This
craft weighs 374 lb. and can be transported by a small car.
It has been included in the Olympic classes, and if in spite
of its cost (about £400) it should become really popular,
then high standards of sailing will be developed by intense
competition among large numbers of helmsmen and we

Running with the tide, and with the wind over our port quarter, we waited for the centre-plate to touch bottom, when we rapidly hauled it up to avoid undue strain on it as we drove ashore. Tony lifted the rudder, spilled some wind from the sails, and ran us firmly aground in the most awkward position for getting away again—with our stern to the tide. I immediately stepped overboard, amidships on the starboard beam, nearest the shore. Standing knee-deep in water and mud I grasped the gunwale firmly near the side stays and pushed the bows round to head into wind —and still farther to head partly into the tide—with the wind fine over the starboard bow. By hauling the boat forward, and then pushing from the starboard quarter, I got her into deeper water, and with a final thrust, scrambled aboard over the stern. My efforts in thrusting from starboard had served not only to push the boat into deep water, but steadily to force her bows round against the tide, to a point where we could beat to windward. Meanwhile, Tony had lowered the rudder-blade, and controlled both mainsheet and jib while Ann was gently lowering the centre-plate and the boat sailed steadily away, close hauled on a starboard tack with the tide providing a strong lift under her lee bow.

We realised that had we been towing the rowing dinghy we could have used it to carry *Whimsy's* anchor out to deep water and then hauled ourselves off. We could have cleared the lee shore by dropping sails, rowing to deep water, and anchoring while we prepared for sailing again, but it was certainly quicker to use our 'emergency action', and though I did carry some mud aboard, we all appreciated that in a real emergency this would be a very minor trouble.

We next sailed across to the weather side of the estuary and beating close hauled to windward on a port tack continued our approach to the shore until our centre-plate touched bottom. While I hauled it clear, Tony let the mainsheet go free, put up the helm and used the jib to help us bear away to deep water where I could lower the

should increase our chances of success in the Olympic Games.

In larger classes, relying on deep ballast keels for their stability, the safety factor is high—if we regard capsizing as 'dangerous'—and the crew is not called upon to act as mobile ballast. Winches take much of the hard work out of hauling, 'sitting out' is unnecessary, and the crew, having no need to move rapidly in balancing the boat on sliding seat or trapeze, may enjoy the comfort of slacks, sweaters and oilskins.

Craft like the Dragon have a tiny cabin providing 'sitting headroom', but accommodation is sufficiently spartan to discourage anything more protracted than racing or day cruising.

The typical 'cruiser' of similar overall length has a deeper body, fuller sections, greater beam generally, higher free-board, built-up cabin sides, standing head room in the saloon, comfortable berths, a galley for cooking, fo'c'sle with sea water w.c., and a tiny auxiliary engine under the cockpit. She provides comfortable accommodation for two or three people to enjoy week-end or summer holiday cruising. For their greater comfort—and some will feel, greater safety—they are prepared to forgo the speed of a racing craft.

The 'ideal' boat—really fast—comfortable, completely safe, and—inexpensive, has not yet been built.

Chapter 10

SIXTH SAILING SESSION

FOR our last day under instruction, the weather was excellent, and we took advantage of the fresh breeze to lend reality to a few practices of points which we might need to know in future.

A lee-shore is the dread of the helmsman sailing a keel boat, especially if the tide is falling. In a sailing boat with a centre-plate there are fewer worries but we felt it wise to be familiar with various means of getting off a lee-shore. Accordingly, we sailed against the tide, with the wind over the starboard quarter on a course that would drive us directly ashore (*Fig. 73*).

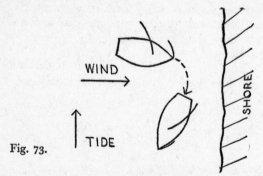

Fig. 73.

As we approached ever closer to the bank, I prepared to lift the centre-plate and the moment we felt it touch bottom, I immediately hauled it up sufficiently to be clear. At the same time Tony put down the helm and hauled in the

94

---

mainsheet while Ann let go the jib and we rounded up into wind to a close hauled course. I lowered the plate progressively as we reached deeper water, and so we found it possible to risk going close to a shore provided we were ready for emergency action. On a second run we deliberately beached our boat (*Fig. 74*).

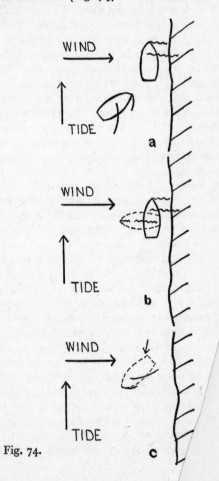

Fig. 74.

plate again. Going aground on a weather shore need cause us no worry in our boat, at any state of the tide.

Throughout our training we have kept the centre-plate lowered on all points of sailing, but now, while running with the wind aft, where we had no need for the lateral resistance of the centre-plate, we hauled it up to reduce surface friction and so increase our speed.

When we take to racing this will be essential, but I can see that if we forget to lower the plate at the end of a run, we are liable to capsize in going about or gybing.

Having all read of craft lying 'hove to' for riding out bad weather at sea, we were anxious to try this, and selected open water near the weather side of the estuary for the purpose. From a close hauled point of sailing with the wind over the port bow we backed the jib firmly to port and eased off the mainsheet very gently to balance the boat. We didn't worry about the tiller at all, but merely backed the jib and lashed it, then adjusted the position of the mainsheet until the boat was making little forward progress, but drifting slowly to loo'ard. *Whimsy* certainly rode quietly in this unusual position, and when we found the correct 'balancing' point for the mainsail, she remained fairly steady with the backed jib forcing her bows away from the wind, and the mainsail having the effect of luffing her up into the wind. An occasional gust would drive her closer, but she invariably swung back again to lie 'hove to'.

Tillers have been known to break, while even the rudder is not immune from damage, and so as a final practice we again found open water and while sailing on a broad reach against the tide took the tiller from the rudder head and sailed the boat merely by balancing the jib and mainsail.

On a broad reach, the effect of the mainsail was stronger than that of the jib and, without the control of the tiller, the boat tended to fly up into the wind. By easing out the mainsheet to the point where the luff of the mainsail was beginning to flutter, we found that we could hold the course we wanted. At the end of our reach we went about by releasing the jib completely and hauling in the mainsail firmly. Again we sailed on a broad reach but in the opposite direction without help from the rudder.

With some practice we found it possible to hold all points from reaching to beating. Running was very much more difficult, while the mainsail was up, but under the jib only *Whimsy* ran quite well with the wind directly astern, or over the quarter, and could be 'steered' to port or starboard by flying the jib to one side or the other.

These practices completed, we returned to our moorings, where we put the Captain aboard the rowing dinghy, then immediately made for our triangular course. The Captain rowed out to join us, and anchored at our gybing point. For the rest of the morning we practised circuits, and finally sailed alone to our mooring buoy, thrilled to know that we *can* now cruise about the estuary without assistance.

We still have much to learn, but if we think carefully we know the action we should take at any time. We can trim our sheets for any point of sailing. We know the rules for avoiding collision. Experience should teach us to think quickly of all these things in advance of the moment when they are necessary. Already we have learnt that in a boat you pay for your mistakes. This payment is generally immediate and painful, but if delayed is none the less certain. The bruised fingers that come from gripping the gunwale while going alongside the dinghy; the sore head from just failing to duck under the boom; and grazed shins that mark the times we tripped over the centre-plate box instead of stepping over it, all serve to drive these points home. In those jobs such as standing on the main thwart and reaching up to clear the wool 'tell-tale'—our apparent wind indicator—we invariably hold firmly with one hand to the mast or to the standing rigging, rigorously obeying the important rule of 'one hand for yourself and one for the boat'.

Our confidence has been built up by sailing under near-ideal conditions, and though it may be a true saying that

'Constant fair winds will never make a sailor', I know that in bad weather we could pay dearly for even a single mistake, and give unnecessary trouble to the local fishermen and lifeboat crew who would come to our aid. Force 3 winds, up to 10 knots, will be ideal for us.

We know that against a force 4 wind—up to 16 knots— we can beat to windward only slowly if a strong tide is also against us, while this wind blowing against the tide will build up waves large enough to throw considerable quantities of water aboard on a beat.

In slightly stronger winds, force 5—up to 21 knots— we'll leave moorings only if the wind is *across* the estuary— and even so we will be well reefed.

Until we've served a reasonable period of apprenticeship, we'll be guided by local advice concerning suitable weather conditions, and we'll postpone the exhilaration of battling against half a gale in the estuary until we know our boat intimately and can react immediately and correctly to all those variable conditions of wind and tide we are now learning to expect.

Meanwhile, with a sound basis of knowledge on which to build by experience, we look forward to many seasons of pleasure, and I'm glad to be assured that 'There's always something more to learn about boats and sailing—nobody knows it all'.

Glossary

ABACK. A sail is *aback* when it is prevented from drawing normally, by having the jib sheet close hauled to windward or the boom of a mainsail held to the weather side. In each case the normal effect of the wind on the sail is reversed. The jib is *backed* to help turn the boat. See page 16.

ABAFT. To the aft side—or astern of. *Abaft the beam* is aft of amidships. See page 41.

ABEAM. To the side—port or starboard; the wind is *abeam* on a reach. See page 18.

ABOUT. To *go*, or *put*, *about*—to sail on the opposite tack. See page 17.

APPARENT WIND. The resultant of the direction and force of the true wind, affected by the course and speed of the boat, and indicated by wool 'tell-tale' or by burgee. See page 15.

A-LEE. To leeward—in the general direction to which the wind blows, e.g. The *helm's a-lee*, in going about. See page 17.

BACK. A wind *backs* when its direction changes against the general arc of the sun's movement—e.g. a change from West to South. It is often a sign of bad weather.

BACK SPLICE. See page 77.

BATTENS. Thin strips of wood or plastic inserted in pockets in the leach (the trailing edge) of the sail to keep it fully extended and help hold its shape. Fully battened sails have several pockets right across from leach to luff.

BEAMY. Broad; said of a boat when her breadth is great in proportion to her length.

BEAR AWAY. To steer the vessel to leeward of her previous course so that her bows *bear away* from the wind direction. See page 20.

BEAT. A course close hauled to windward. See page 26.

BELAY. To make fast the end of a rope by turning it round a cleat or belaying pin. See pages 20, 23.

BEND A SAIL. To fix a sail into position ready to haul up for sailing. See page 13.

BERMUDIAN RIG. Having a tall mast to carry a triangular mainsail. See page 54.

BIGHT. The loop formed by a rope when a knot or hitch is being made. See page 76.

BLOCK AND TACKLE. A system of two pulley blocks—to increase mechanical power or purchase.

BOLT ROPE. The rope surrounding a sail, and to which the canvas is sewn.

BOOM. A spar that extends the foot of the sail.

BOTTLE SCREW. A brass tube with right-hand thread at one end and left hand thread at the other. In each end is a solid brass screw, to shackle to rigging and chain plate respectively. Turning the main tube tightens or slackens the rigging.

BOWLINE. See page 80.

BROACH TO. To bear away so much, when sailing free, as to bring the boat nearly broadside on to the wind.

BROAD REACH. Sailing with the wind over the beam.

BULKHEADS. Partitions dividing a vessel into sections.

BURGEE. A small flag often with Club colours, flown from masthead and pivoted sensitively to give an indication of the apparent wind direction. See page 15.

CARVEL. Method of building in which the outer planking is fixed edge to edge. See page 62.

CATAMARAN. A twin-hulled or multi-hulled craft. See page 65.

CENTRE-PLATE. An iron or wooden plate generally rectangular in shape, normally housed in its case or trunk above the keel of the boat. It is pivoted near the lower front corner. When the free end is lowered to hang under the boat, it offers sideways resistance. An iron plate increases stability. See page 51.

CHAIN-PLATE. A strip or plate of metal fixed to the top planks on the side of a boat to take the strain of the side-stays.

CLEW. The lower aft corner of a fore-and-aft sail. The jib sheets are fixed to the *clew*.

CLINKER BUILT. Construction in which outside planking overlaps. See page 62.

CLOSE HAULED. Sailing as close as possible to the direction of the wind—with sheets hauled in. See page 26.

CLOVE HITCH. See page 74.

COMMON WHIPPING. See page 78.

COUNTER. See page 61.

CRINGLE. A rope eye enclosing a metal thimble, spliced into the bolt rope of a sail through which a reef earing is rove.

CROWN OF AN ANCHOR. Where the arms and shank join.

CRUTCH. A wooden support for the boom when the mainsail is furled.

CUTTER. A craft with two triangular sails in front of a single mainsail. See 'Foresail'. See page 56.

DAGGER-PLATE. See page 58.

DEADWOODS. Large blocks of wood, supporting the main framework at the juncture of stem with keel and keel with stern post.

DINGHY. The smallest of a yacht's boats. A small pulling boat. A small sailing boat.

DISPLACEMENT. The weight of water that a boat displaces when she is afloat.

EARING. A rope which passes through the cringle of a sail and serves to reef it.

EYE SPLICE. See page 76.

FAIR-LEAD. A block or a guide through which a rope

passes, e.g. a jib sheet *fair-lead*, or a *fair-lead* for mooring rope or chain.

FALL OF A ROPE.　The loose end or part to be hauled.

FATHOM.　6 feet.

FIGURE OF EIGHT.　A knot generally used in the end of jib sheets, to prevent the windward sheet escaping from its fair-lead.　See page 74.

FISHERMAN'S BEND.　See page 75.

FLUKES.　The barbs at the extremities of an anchor's arms.

FOREREACH.　To travel ahead in stays—by reason of momentum or 'way' gained previously.　See pages 21, 38, 48.

FORESAIL.　In the case of a single-masted boat, the *foresail* is the triangular sail carried in front of the mast.　A single *foresail* or headsail, as in a sloop, is generally called the jib.　In the case of a cutter with two headsails, the outer one is called the jib and the inner is called the *foresail*.　On a schooner (see page 57) the fore and aft sail abaft the fore-mast is called the *foresail*.

FREE.　Sailing on a course where it is possible to luff up —closer to the wind direction—or to bear away still more. See page 28.

FREEBOARD.　Height of deck above water line.

FULL AND BYE.　With sails well filled—able to luff closer if necessary.　See page 28.

GAFF RIGGED.　Having a quadrilateral sail hung from a spar called the *gaff*.　See page 54.

GAFF.　The spar from which the quadrilateral-shaped sail is supported.　See page 54.

GARBOARD STRAKES.　The planks nearest the keel.

GIMBALS.　A contrivance consisting of a metal ring pivoted to swing freely, inside which a compass, lamp or Primus, similarly pivoted but at right-angles to the outer pivots, is hung.　The compass, etc., will maintain a level position despite the movement of the vessel.

GROUND TACKLE. The anchor and cables used in anchoring a vessel.

GUNWALE. The top of the side planking of a boat.

GYBE. When sailing with the wind abaft the beam, to turn so that the wind comes on the opposite quarter, causing the boom to be 'blown' across the boat. See page 34.

Gybe all Standing—when this manœuvre is unexpected and uncontrolled.

HALF HITCHES. See page 73.

HALYARDS. Rope of manilla, hemp, etc., or of wire, used for hoisting sails.

HEEL. To lean sideways or list. The heel of the mast is the foot, or the part that is stepped on keel or deck.

HELM DOWN. When the helm or tiller is put over in the direction towards which the wind is blowing.

HELM UP. When the helm or tiller is put over in the direction from which the wind is blowing.

HORSE. Generally a length of metal rod fixed above the stern of the boat, and provided with a jockey pulley block or traveller that can run freely from end to end and through which the main sheet (see 'Sheets') is rove.

HOVE TO. See page 97.

IN IRONS. A vessel is *in irons* when she is in the wind's eye, and, having lost all headway, will not go off on either tack, under her own momentum. See page 69.

IN STAYS. See 'Stays'. See page 69.

JIB. A triangular-shaped foresail, or head sail.

KEDGE. A small anchor. *To kedge*, is to drag, or warp a vessel along with rope and kedge, or to anchor temporarily with such tackle.

KEEL. The spine of the vessel—as the timbers are ribs. The main fore and aft member on which the boat is built. Ballast in the form of a *fin keel* or *false keel* of iron fixed below the actual *wooden keel*, provides stability as well as lateral resistance.

KETCH. A boat with a mizzen mast stepped forward of the steering gear. See page 58.

KICKING STRAP. A wire or stout cord fixed from the boom to the foot of the mast to hold down the boom when gybing.

LEE BOARD. See page 59.

LEE-HELM. A vessel is said to *carry lee-helm* when she has a tendency to bear away from the wind, and the tiller has to be kept down in order to counteract this. A well-designed boat with her normal sails set should not have *lee-helm*.

LEE SHORE. A shore towards which the wind is blowing. See page 94.

LEEWAY. The movement of a boat sideways through the water in the direction to which the wind is blowing.

LIST. Said of a boat when she leans sideways, for instance to leeward by reason of the pressure of the wind.

L.O.A. = Length over all.

LOO'ARD (Leeward). The *leeward* side of the boat, away from the wind; the general direction towards which the wind blows.

LUFF. Leading edge of the sail.
To *Luff Up* is to steer closer to the wind direction. See page 20.

L.W.L. = Length of Load Water Line, i.e. when boat is fully loaded.

MARK. An indication or turning point on a course. Some object to steer for.

MIZZEN. The small sail supported on the *mizzen mast*—stepped aft of the mainmast. See page 58.

PAINTER. Light rope fixed in bows of dinghy for making fast.

PEAK. The top of the sail.

PORT. The left-hand side of the boat as you look forward.

PORT TACK. With the wind over the port bow. See page 26.

PREVENTER. An additional rope or wire placed to assist another one in supporting a strain, e.g. a *preventer backstay* assists the backstay. See 'Stays'.

PURCHASE. An arrangement of ropes and pulleys by which mechanical power is gained. See 'Block and Tackle'.

QUARTER. The after part of a vessel's side.

REACHING. Sailing with wind abeam. To sail *on a broad reach* is to sail with wind slightly abaft the beam.

REEFING. To reduce the area of a sail by rolling or tying up a portion of it at the foot. See page 49.

RIGGING—RUNNING. Rope and/or wire that hoists or controls sails—e.g. sheets and halyards.

RIGGING—STANDING. Wire stays that support the mast, e.g. forestay—sidestays—backstays, etc. They are adjusted only occasionally and are not moved while normally working a boat. Bottle screws are generally incorporated for making adjustments to length.

RUDDER PINTLES. The metal pins on which the rudder hangs and swings.

RUDDER-PLATE. The thin wooden or metal blade of the rudder pivoted so that it can be lifted in shallow water, or lowered in deep water.

RUN. The *run* of a vessel is the after part of her underwater sections, generally narrowing and lifting up to the stern.

To let go a halyard '*by the run*' is to let it go altogether, not ease it out gently.

RUNNING. Sailing with the wind aft. See page 41.

SAG. To *sag to leeward* is to drift with the wind—to make leeway.

SCHOONER. See page 58.

SHAKE UP. To luff up for a short time without losing a vessel's way until the sails shake, when with the pressure of wind off them the crew can take a pull on the halyards or purchases if these have stretched.

SHANK. The long body or stem of an anchor connecting the arms with the stock.

SHEER. The shape of a deck line from bow to stern as it appears in a side view. *Reverse Sheer* or *Hogged Sheer*—See page 60.

SHEETS. Ropes used to trim sails, i.e. to control their position—e.g. *jib sheets* fixed to clew of sail, to control it; *mainsheet* controlling the boom carrying the mainsail.

SLOOP. A boat with two sails—mainsail and jib. See page 55.

SPAR. A mast, a boom, or a gaff that gives support to a sail.

SPLICE. See page 75.

STANDING PART OF A ROPE. The part already made fast to something.

STARBOARD. The right-hand side of the boat as you look forward.

STARBOARD TACK. With the wind over the starboard bow.

STAYS. Ropes supporting a mast, e.g. *forestay*, *sidestays* and *backstays*. See 'Rigging'.

In Stays—when a boat is in the wind's eye while going about from one tack to another. See page 69.

STEM. The main piece of timber in the bows, into which fore and aft planking is fitted.

STERNBOARD. When a boat is heading into wind, but moving backwards. See page 69.

STIFF. A boat is *stiff* when she can carry her sail without listing unduly. She has ample stability.

STOCK. The moveable cross-bar at the upper end of an anchor.

STOP. A binding, e.g. with whipping cotton or fine yarn to prevent a rope from unlaying. See page 76.

STROP. An eye of rope or wire spliced round a block.

SWIGGING ON A ROPE. See page 23.

TABERNACLE.   A mast-step fixed on deck, in which the mast is pivoted for ease of lowering, e.g. to negotiate bridges on inland waterways.

TACK.   The lower fore corner of a sail.

TACKING.   A zigzag course for making progress against the wind.   See '*Port tack*', '*Starboard tack*'.   See page 26.

THIMBLE.   A metal ring, with a concave outer edge, round which a rope can be spliced.   The metal protects the rope from chafing.   See page 75.

THWARTS.   The 'seats'—heavy planks of timber that brace the boat cross-wise.

TIDE RODE.   A boat is *tide rode* when lying anchored or moored with bows to tide, she is affected by the strength of the tide more than by the wind.   See page 40.

TIMBERS.   In a small boat strips of oak, riveted to the inside of all planking, and running from the top plank on one side, across the keel, and so to the top plank on the opposite side.   Sometimes called the ribs of the boat.

TOPPING LIFT.   A rope passing through a block or sheave at the mast head, to sustain the weight of the boom. By hauling on this the boom is raised to a position slightly higher than for normal sailing; used as a temporary measure while the mainsail is hoisted, to avoid unnecessary drag by the weight of the boom.

VEER.   A wind change, where the direction has moved in the same arc as the sun, i.e. clockwise—e.g. a change of wind from East to South.   Generally a good weather sign.

WAIST.   The midships section of a vessel.

WEARING SHIP.   See page 43.

WEATHER.   The direction from which the wind blows. The side of the boat that is to windward.

WEATHER-HELM.   A ship is said to *carry weather-helm* when she has a tendency to come up into the wind, and requires the tiller to be kept to windward so as to counteract this. As a fault, it is much preferable to *lee-helm*.

WIND RODE.   A boat is *wind rode* when anchored or

moored with bows to wind—affected by wind strength more than by tide strength.   See page 40.

WENDING.   See page 46.

WHIP.   A purchase formed by a rope rove through a single block.

WHIPPING.   See page 78.

WINDWARD.   The general direction from which the wind is blowing.

YAW.   When a vessel goes off her course first to one side then to the other.

YAWL.   A boat having a mainsail with two triangular sails in front of it, and a mizzen stepped in the stern.   See page 58.

Park, W. D.
(S) Sailing. A